Broadman Comments
September-November 1998

BROADMAN COMMENTS

September-November 1998

13 User-Friendly Bible Study Lessons

ROBERT J. DEAN

WILLIAM E. ANDERSON

JAMES E. TAULMAN

BROADMAN
& HOLMAN
PUBLISHERS

Nashville, Tennessee

This material was published first in *Broadman Comments, 1998–1999*

© Copyright 1998 • Broadman and Holman Publishers
Nashville, Tennessee
All rights reserved

ISBN: 0–8054–1758–3

The Outlines of the International Sunday School Lessons, Uniform Series, are copyrighted by the Committee on the Uniform Series and are used by permission.

Dewey Decimal Classification: 268.61
Subject Heading: SUNDAY SCHOOL LESSONS—COMMENTARIES

Broadman Comments *is published quarterly by Broadman & Holman Publishers, 127 Ninth Avenue, North, Nashville, Tennessee 37234*

When ordered with other church literature, it sells for $5.99 per quarter. Second class postage paid at Nashville, Tennessee

ISSN: 0068–2721

POSTMASTER: Send address change to *Broadman Comments*,
Customer Service Center, 127 Ninth Avenue, North
Nashville, Tennessee 37234

Library of Congress Catalog Card Number: 45–437
Printed in the United States of America

WRITERS

STUDYING THE BIBLE

Robert J. Dean continues the theological traditions of *Broadman Comments* while adding his own fresh insights. Dean is retired from the Baptist Sunday School Board and is a Th.D. graduate of New Orleans Seminary.

APPLYING THE BIBLE

William E. Anderson has been pastor of Calvary Baptist Church, Clearwater, Florida, since 1975. Calvary's weekly services are telecast on various local stations and by satellite over Christian Network, Inc., on the Dish Network.

TEACHING THE BIBLE

James E. Taulman is a freelance writer in Nashville, Tennessee. Prior to that, Taulman was an editor of adult Sunday school materials for the Baptist Sunday School Board.

Scripture passages are from the authorized King James Version of the Bible.

Contents

GOD CALLS A PEOPLE TO FAITHFUL LIVING

UNIT 1   GOD FASHIONS A PEOPLE
Sept. 6 — God's Creation Marred by Sin.................. 3
Sept. 13 — Celebrate: God Delivers a People from Slavery 11
Sept. 20 — What God Expects........................... 19
Sept. 27 — Remembering What God Has Done 27

UNIT II   GOD LEADS IN TIMES OF CHANCE
Oct. 4 — Cycle of Sin and Judgment 35
Oct. 11 — From Judges to Kings 43
Oct. 18 — Jeroboam's Sin.............................. 51

UNIT III   GOD WORKS THROUGH PEOPLE
Oct. 25 — The Work of Prophets 59
Nov. 1 — Courage to Speak for God 67
Nov. 8 — Writers of Songs 75

UNIT IV   GOD JUDGES AND RENEWS
Nov. 15 — False Hopes and Judgment 82
Nov. 22 — God's Vision for Exiles...................... 90
Nov. 29 — Renewal and Worship 97

Cycle of 1998–2004

1998–1999	1999–2000	2000–2001	2001–2002	2002–2003	2003–2004
Old Testament Survey	Exodus Leviticus Numbers Deuteronomy Joshua	Judges 1, 2 Samuel 1 Chronicles 1 Kings 1–11 2 Chronicles 1–9	Parables Miracles Sermon on the Mount	2 Kings 18–25 2 Chronicles 29–36 Jeremiah Lamentations Ezekiel Habakkuk Zephaniah	James 1, 2 Peter 1, 2, 3 John Jude
New Testament Survey	Matthew	Luke	Isaiah 9; 11; 40–66; Ruth Jonah Nahum	Personalities of the NT	Christmas Esther Job Ecclesiastes Song of Solomon
John	1, 2 Corinthians	Acts	Romans Galatians	Mark	The Cross 1, 2 Thessalonians Revelation
Genesis	Ephesians Philippians Colossians Philemon	1 Kings 12– 2 Kings 17 2 Chronicles 10–28 Isaiah 1–39 Amos Hosea Micah	Psalms Proverbs	Ezra Nehemiah Daniel Joel Obadiah Haggai Zechariah Malachi	Hebrews 1, 2 Timothy Titus

God Calls a People to Faithful Living

SEPTEMBER
OCTOBER
NOVEMBER

INTRODUCTION

1998

The International Sunday School Lessons are designed in six-year cycles. Each cycle seeks to include some lessons from all parts of the Bible. Most quarters consist of studies in one or more Bible books. Some Old Testament and some New Testament studies are provided each year. At least one study each year is on the life and ministry of Jesus Christ. Since most of the passages selected for study vary from cycle to cycle, no cycle merely repeats the previous cycle.

This is the first quarter in a new six-year cycle. The cycle is printed below so you can see how it looks. The first quarter is a survey of the Old Testament.

Unit I, "God Fashions a People," focuses on the coming of sin, deliverance from Egypt, the Ten Commandments, and the conquest of Canaan.

Unit II, "God Leads in Times of Change," focuses on the cycle of sin during the period of the judges, the transition from judges to kings, and the evil influence of the sin of Jeroboam I.

Unit III, "God Works Through People," focuses on a nonwriting prophet (Elisha), a writing prophet (Amos), and on Psalm 73.

Unit IV, "God Judges and Renews," focuses on the final days of Judah (Jeremiah), the Babylonian exile (Ezekiel), and the restoration to the holy land (Ezra).

Nine Periods of Old Testament History

1. **Beginnings:** From creation untill the scattering of humanity after the tower of Babel
2. **Patriarchs:** From the call of Abraham until Jacob and his family settled in Egypt
3. **Exodus:** From the oppression in Egypt until the death of Moses
4. **Conquest:** From the call to cross the Jordan River until the death of Joshua
5. **Judges:** From the death of Joshua until just before the birth of Samuel
6. **United Kingdom:** From the birth of Samuel until the death of Solomon
7. **Divided Kingdom:** From the division of the kingdom under Rehoboam until the fall of Judah to Babylon
8. **Exile:** From the carrying of the Jews to Babylon until the edict of Cyrus allowing them to return to Jerusalem
9. **Restoration:** From Cyrus's edict through the time of Malachi

God's Creation Marred by Sin

September 6 1998

Background Passage: Genesis 3
Focal Passage: Genesis 3:1–13

Genesis 1–3 contains truths that are foundational to biblical revelation. Two truths are revealed about the doctrine of man; and a third is anticipated:
1. Genesis 1–2 presents humans as the highest of God's good creation.
2. Genesis 3 shows that humans are sinners.
3. Genesis 3 also anticipates a truth emphasized in later biblical revelation: People can be redeemed by God's grace.

▶**Study Aim:** *To identify basic biblical teachings about temptation and sin.*

STUDYING THE BIBLE

OUTLINE AND SUMMARY
   I. Temptation (Gen. 3:1–5)
      1. The tempter (3:1a)
      2. The temptation (3:1b–5)
   II. Sin (Gen. 3:6–13)
      1. When temptation becomes sin (3:6)
      2. Guilt and grace (3:7–10)
      3. Confrontation and excuse-making (3:11–13)
   III. Punishment (Gen. 3:14–24)
      1. Curses of sin (3:14–19)
      2. Driven from the garden (3:20–24)

The tempter came as a clever distorter of truth (3:1a). He used questions, denials of God's word, and half-truths to suggest that God was trying to keep Adam and Eve from experiencing all of life (3:1b–5). The temptation of the attractive tree became sin when Adam and Eve ate of its fruit (3:6). Shame, guilt, and fear caused them to hide from God when He came seeking them (3:7–10). When God confronted them, Adam and Eve blamed someone other than themselves (3:11–13). God announced punishments in the form of curses (3:14–19). God clothed the guilty pair and excluded them from the garden and the tree of life (3:20–24).

I. Temptation (Gen. 3:1–5)
1. The tempter (3:1a)

> 1 Now the serpent was more subtil than any beast of the field which the LORD God had made.

We know from later revelation that the tempter was none other than "the Devil, and Satan" (Rev. 12:9). The word translated "subtil" means "crafty."

September 6, 1998

God Himself is good. He never tempts anyone to do evil (Jas. 1:13). However, God, who created all things, chose to create human beings with freedom to choose. This made evil a possibility. Why did God allow freedom of choice? He could have made creatures who were programmed always to obey. He apparently made us free because only free beings can choose to love God.

2. The temptation (3:1b–5)

1 And he said unto the woman, Yea, hath God said, Ye shall not eat of every tree of the garden?

2 And the woman said unto the serpent, We may eat of the fruit of the trees of the garden:

3 But of the fruit of the tree which is in the midst of the garden, God hath said, Ye shall not eat of it, neither shall ye touch it, lest ye die.

4 And the serpent said unto the woman, Ye shall not surely die:

5 For God doth know that in the day ye eat thereof, then your eyes shall be opened, and ye shall be as gods, knowing good and evil.

The serpent asked the question in verse 1 in order to sow the seeds of doubt. Eve had been focused on the rich abundance of what God had provided for her and Adam. The serpent's question caused her to focus on the one thing denied to them. This is one of the characteristics of temptation: *Temptation blinds us to the good blessings of God and focuses our attention on the sins against which God warns us.*

Eve's response hints that she was beginning to nibble at the tempter's bait. She stated the words of God in their most restricted form (compare Gen. 2:16–17). The tempter quickly denied that God really intended to kill them if they ate the forbidden fruit. This is a second characteristic of temptation: *Temptation denies that God will punish sin as drastically as He warns.*

The tempter told Eve that God did not want Adam and Eve to know or experience both good and evil. He implied that only by experiencing both good and evil could they experience life at its fullest. Thus, the tempter implied that God did not have their best interests at heart. This is a third characteristic of temptation: *Temptation promises a fuller experience of life than we have known.* Closely related is a fourth characteristic: *Temptation implies that God cannot be trusted because He tries to keep us from experiencing all that life has to offer.*

God feared, said the tempter, that they would become like God. The word translated "gods" is the same word translated "God" elsewhere in Genesis 1–3. It is a plural form that can mean "gods" (Gen. 31:30), but it is also the usual word for God in the Bible. Satan tempted them to believe that they could be their own gods if they asserted themselves and ate the forbidden fruit. The fifth characteristic of temptation is this: *Temptation appeals to pride and the self-centered desire to live our lives as we please without God's narrow prohibitions.*

September 6, 1998

Five Characteristics of Temptation
1. Temptation blinds us to the good blessings of God and focuses our attention on the sins against which God warns us.
2. Temptation denies that God will punish sin as drastically as He warns.
3. Temptation promises a fuller experience of life than we have known.
4. Temptation implies that God cannot be trusted because He tries to keep us from experiencing all that life has to offer.
5. Temptation appeals to pride and the self-centered desire to live our lives as we please without God's narrow prohibitions.

II. Sin (Gen. 3:6–13)
1. When temptation becomes sin (3:6)

> **6 And when the woman saw that the tree was good for food, and that it was pleasant to the eyes, and a tree to be desired to make one wise, she took of the fruit thereof, and did eat, and gave also unto her husband with her; and he did eat.**

In light of the tempter's clever words, Eve now saw the tree of the knowledge of good and evil through different eyes. The fruit looked especially delicious. The tree was attractive to look at. And most of all, the tempter had promised that eating the forbidden fruit would make her wise. So she took the fruit and ate it. Nothing is said about what she said to Adam. All we are told is that he also ate the forbidden fruit.

Temptation is not sin until people give in to the temptation. Everyone is tempted. It is common to the human race (1 Cor. 10:13). Even Jesus was tempted, but He did not sin (Heb. 4:15). At what point does temptation become sin? If the sin is an action, the person has given in to the temptation at least by the time of the action. If the sin is an attitude, the point of surrender is not as easy to pinpoint; however, if people continue to flirt with temptation, they often give in to it.

Why was it wrong for Adam and Eve to eat a piece of fruit from a tree? Eating the forbidden fruit was only the outward symptom of a deadly sin. In their case, eating the forbidden fruit was an act of distrust in God, disobedience to God, and turning from God to live life on their own terms. All of these are aspects of the biblical definition of sin. *Sin is distrust in God that results in disobedience of God's commandments and in turning from God to live according to our own way.*

The Bible says that everyone except Jesus has followed in the footsteps of Adam and Eve. As Isaiah 53:6 puts it: "All we like sheep have gone astray; we have turned every one to his own way." Although sin has moral aspects, sin has to do with our relationship with God. *Anything that separates people from God is sin.*

2. Guilt and grace (3:7–10)

> **7 And the eyes of them both were opened, and they knew that they were naked; and they sewed fig leaves together, and made themselves aprons.**

September 6, 1998

> 8 And they heard the voice of the LORD God walking in the garden in the cool of the day: and Adam and his wife hid themselves from the presence of the LORD God amongst the trees of the garden.
> 9 And the LORD God called unto Adam, and said unto him, Where art thou?
> 10 And he said, I heard thy voice in the garden, and I was afraid, because I was naked and I hid myself.

Adam and Eve had been living in harmony with God and with each other. After sin came, openness and honesty were exchanged for shame and guilt. They suddenly became aware of their nakedness. When God came near, rather than rushing to greet Him, they hid from Him. The tempter had been only partially right. When they ate the fruit, they experienced evil for themselves, but this did not lead to a better life. Instead, sin separated them from God.

Genesis 3 shows two reasons why sin separates from God. One reason is because that is what sin is—turning our backs on God, going our own way, hiding from Him. The other reason, which is illustrated in God driving them from the garden, is because sinful people cannot have fellowship with a holy God. Here is another characteristic of sin: *Sin is separation from God that results in fear and guilt.*

Verse 9 is the first hint of hope for sinful humanity. God came looking for Adam and Eve. God's question in verse 9 does not mean that God did not know Adam's location. He knew Adam was hiding and where he was hiding. The question shows that God was seeking them, even though they had turned away from God. They may have expected God to come in a thunderbolt of wrath to strike them dead on the spot. They deserved no less. However, God came seeking them.

Genesis 3:8–9 announces the central message of the rest of the Bible. On one hand, the Bible records the dark record of human sin as sinners who turned from, ran from, and hid from God; but it also tells of God in love setting out to save sinners. God sent His Son to seek and save the lost (Luke 19:10; see also Luke 15:1–10).

3. Confrontation and excuse-making (3:11–13)

> 11 And he said, Who told thee that thou wast naked? Hast thou eaten of the tree, whereof I commanded thee that thou shouldest not eat?
> 12 And the man said, The woman whom thou gavest to be with me, she gave me of the tree, and I did eat.
> 13 And the LORD God said unto the woman, What is this that thou hast done? And the woman said, The serpent beguiled me, and I did eat.

After asking several questions, God confronted Adam with the question about eating the forbidden fruit. Adam admitted that he had eaten the fruit, but he did not admit his personal accountability. Adam blamed Eve in a way that suggested God was also to blame. Notice the words "the woman whom thou gavest." In essence, Adam said: "My wife is to blame, not me. And God, You are the one who made her to be my wife."

When God asked Eve what she had done, she replied by blaming the tempter for deceiving her. This is characteristic of sin: *Sinners often refuse to confess their own responsibility for their sins; instead, they blame others, Satan, and even God.* Closely related is this fact: *Sin separates not only from God but also from others, including members of our own families.* Adam and Eve had lived in harmony, trust, and love. Now they were blaming each other. Their sin had disrupted their own relationship. This terrible characteristic of sin is powerfully reinforced in Genesis 4, when the first child born to Adam and Eve murdered his brother.

III. Punishment (Gen. 3:14–24)
1. Curses of sin (3:14–19)

Sin blighted the lives of the first pair and their descendants. God's good earth was affected by the curses. Work, which had been a part of the good creation (Gen. 2:15), became grinding toil (3:17–19). Pain became the woman's lot (3:16). The curse on the serpent is another ray of hope in the midst of the curses. Christians see Jesus Christ as the fulfillment of the promise about the woman's seed whose heel would be bruised by the serpent but who would crush the serpent's head (3:14–15).

2. Driven from the garden (3:20–24)

The fact that God clothed the guilty pair is a sign of His grace (3:20–21). God excluded Adam and Eve from the garden and left angels to guard its entrance (3:22–24). The primary message is that sin separates sinners from the holy God and the eternal life He wants to give them. However, there is at least a hint of hope in God not destroying the sinners or the tree of life. Revelation 22:2 pictures redeemed people in a new creation with the tree of life.

SUMMARY OF BIBLE TRUTHS

1. The tempter seeks to undermine our trust that God wants the best for us.
2. Sin is basically distrust and disobedience to God.
3. Sin separates from God and alienates from other people.
4. Sin's consequences are not freedom and fulfillment, but shame and guilt.
5. Sinners often refuse to accept personal accountability for their sins.
6. Sinners seek to hide from God, but God seeks to provide salvation and reconciliation.

APPLYING THE BIBLE

1. Guilty! One day in September 1972, a man stood on a busy street in Chicago. As people walked by and met his gaze, he would point his finger in their face and shout one word: "Guilty!" Then, he would turn and say the same thing to another passerby. People responded strangely. "They would stare at him, hesitate, look away, look at each other, and then at him again; then hurriedly continue on their ways. One man, turn-

September 6, 1998

ing to another who was my informant, exclaimed, 'But how did *he* know?'"[1] But, of course, that is the safest guess in the universe! Guilt is a universal fact. One need never ask, "Do you feel guilty?" Sigmund Freud said guilt is the "most important problem in the evolution of culture." I'm not sure about that, but I am sure that it is a problem we all have.

2. Separation and alienation. Sin separates us from God and alienates us from other people. Three Old Testament passages fix this in our memory:

- Amos 3:3: "Can two walk together except they be agreed?"
- Isaiah 59:1–2: "Behold, the LORD'S hand is not shortened, that it cannot save: neither his ear heavy, that it cannot hear. But your iniquities have separated between you and your God, and your sins have hid his face from you, that he will not hear."
- Numbers 14:42–45 describes how the disobedient people of God attempted to go to the promised land without God's blessing and presence. God separated Himself from them because of their sin, and they were defeated in battle immediately. Joshua and Caleb had said twice that the Lord would not go with them (vv. 42 and 43). And He didn't. Thus, the defeat. Both for them and for us!

3. Law and order. Former Chicago mayor Richard Daley once said, "As long as I am mayor of Chicago, there will be law and order in Chicago." But, of course, since Genesis 3, no city on earth has experienced total law and order—precisely because of what happened in Genesis 3. That is the explanation of evil in the universe!

4. Sin costs! According to Benjamin Franklin, "We are taxed twice as much by our idleness, three times as much by our pride, and four times as much by our folly; and from these taxes the commissioner cannot ease or deliver us."[2]

5. Are we machines? When asked to define a human being, the engineer-architect-philosopher Buckminster Fuller said that man is "a self-balancing, 28-jointed adapter-base biped. . . . the whole complex mechanism guided with exquisite precision from a turret in which are located telescopic and microscopic self-registering and recording range-finders, a spectroscope, etc., the turret control being closely allied with an air conditioning intake-and-exhaust, and a main fuel intake."[3] But there is no mention in all that of the chief characteristic of all humans—the capacity (which no machine has) to disobey God—and to feel the resulting guilt!

6. Only man. A boy once said to a mountain:
I am greater than you, tho' such a dot;
I can think and pray but you cannot.
Only man, of all creation, feels guilt. Or needs to!

7. Resisting sin. Maybe the profoundest sentence I have ever read about what happened in Genesis 3 is this one from Leonardo da Vinci: "It is easier to resist at the beginning than at the end."

8. On the light side.
- "Every morning is the dawn of a new error."

- The trouble is, we keep on sinning!
- Can sin be solved? "I don't have a solution to the problem, but I sure do admire the problem!"

10. Think about it! Are you like Eve, enticing to sin? Or are you like Adam, following into sin?

TEACHING THE BIBLE

- *Main Idea:* Sin has marred all of God's creation.
- *Suggested Teaching Aim:* To lead adults to accept God's provision to escape the penalties of sin

A TEACHING OUTLINE

God's Creation Marred by Sin (Genesis 3:1–24)
1. *Temptation (3:1–5)*
2. *Sin (3:6–13)*
3. *Punishment (3:14–24)*

Introduce the Bible Study

Make the following quarter poster

God Fashions a People

God's Creation Marred by Sin	September 6
Celebrate: God Delivers a People from Slavery	September 13
What God Expects	September 20
Remembering What God Has Done	September 27
Cycle of Sin and Judgment	October 4
From Judges to Kings	October 11
Jeroboam's Sin	October 18
The Work of Prophets	October 25
Courage to Speak for God	November 1
Writers of Songs	November 8
False Hopes and Judgment	November 15
God's Vision for Exiles	November 22
Renewal and Worship	November 29

Display this all quarter. Cut an arrow out of brightly colored paper and place it beside each lesson each week.

Read "Guilty!" in "Applying the Bible" to introduce the Bible study. Ask, Do you agree that guilt is a problem we all have? Why?

Search for Biblical Truth

On a chalkboard write "1. Temptation (3:1–5)." Ask a volunteer to read Genesis 3:1–5. Ask: How is the serpent related to the devil and

September 6 1998

Satan mentioned in the rest of the Bible? (Same.) Why did God make us free to be able to respond to Him or to reject Him? (Only free beings can choose to love God.) What was the purpose of the serpent's sly question in 3:1? (Sow seeds of doubt.) What advantage would knowing "evil" have for Adam and Eve? (None, but they thought it would have some.) Share the list of five characteristics of temptation in "Studying the Bible." (You might want to copy these and ask a member to read them.)

On the chalkboard write "2. Sin (3:6–13)." Ask a volunteer to read 3:6–13. Ask: Why do you think Eve and Adam ate the fruit? What did eating the fruit symbolize? (Outward symbol of a deadly sin.) Was the tempter right in what he promised Eve? (Partially; they experienced evil but it did not lead to better life.) How did sin affect Adam and Eve's relationship with God? (They hid.) How did sin affect God's relationship with Adam and Eve? (He sought them.) What is one basic similarity in Adam's and Eve's response to God? (Blamed others; Adam blamed Eve and God; Eve blamed snake.) Share the list of five characteristics of sin mentioned in "Studying the Bible."

On the chalkboard, write: "3. Punishment (Gen. 3:14–24)." Ask a volunteer to read Genesis 3:14–24. Use the material in "Studying the Bible" to summarize briefly these verses.

Use the six Bible truths in the "Summary" to present a brief lecture summarizing the truths of the lesson.

Give the Truth a Personal Focus

Ask, How are we like Adam and Eve? Ask members to think of situations in their lives when they have listened to the tempter instead of to God. What problems did this cause? How can they learn from the experience?

Ask, What was God's initial response to Adam and Eve's sin? (Sought them, called to them.) How does God's response to our sin differ? (He still seeks us.) How does He do this? (Sent Christ, Holy Spirit calls.)

Close in prayer that all will accept the salvation and reconciliation God provides.

---

1. Karl Menninger, *Whatever Became of Sin?* (New York: Bantam, 1978), 2.
2. Cited in *The Great American Bathroom Book,* vol. 1 (Salt Lake City: Compact Classics, 1991), 581.
3. Ibid., 579.

Celebrate: God Delivers a People from Slavery

September 13 1998

Background Passages: Exodus 2:23–25; 5:1–2; 11:1–8; 12:29–32; 15:1–2, 19–21

Focal Passages: Exodus 2:23–25; 5:1–2; 12:29–32; 15:1–2

The deliverance from Egypt is one of the most important events of the Old Testament. Later Old Testament writings referred to the Exodus as the proof of God's special love for and choice of Israel to be His people. The cross and resurrection of Jesus are comparable events for Christians (1 Cor. 5:7).

▶**Study Aim:** *To explain why the Exodus was a divine deliverance, not a human escape.*

STUDYING THE BIBLE

OUTLINE AND SUMMARY
  I. God Remembers His Covenant (Exod. 2:23–25)
     1. Cries of oppressed people (2:23)
     2. God's response (2:24–25)
  II. The Lord Confronts Pharaoh (Exod. 5:1–2)
     1. The Lord's demand (5:1)
     2. Pharaoh's defiance (5:2)
  III. The Lord Delivers Israel (Exod. 11:1–8; 12:29–32)
     1. The final plague (11:1–8; 12:29–30)
     2. Pharaoh's reaction (12:31–32)
  IV. Israel Celebrates Deliverance (Exod. 15:1–2, 19–21)
     1. Deliverance at the Red Sea (15:19)
     2. Israel praises the Lord (15:1–2, 20–21)

The cries of the Israelites in Egypt were heard by God (2:23). He prepared to fulfill His covenant to return Israel to the promised land (2:24–25). Speaking through Moses and Aaron, the Lord demanded that Pharaoh let God's people go (5:1). Pharaoh defiantly denied knowing the Lord and refused to obey Him (5:2). The final plague on Egypt was the death of the firstborn (11:1–8; 12:29–30). Pharaoh ordered the Israelites to leave Egypt as God had demanded (12:31–32). When Pharaoh's army pursued the Israelites, the Lord delivered His people at the Red Sea (15:19). Moses, Miriam, and the people exalted the Lord in song (15:1–2, 20–21).

I. God Remembers His Covenant (Exod. 2:23–25)

1. Cries of oppressed people (2:23)

23 And it came to pass in process of time, that the king of Egypt died: and the children of Israel sighed by reason of the bondage, and they cried, and their cry came up unto God by reason of the bondage.

September 13, 1998

Verses 23–25 form a conclusion to Exodus 1–2 and a bridge to the events of the following chapters. Exodus 2:23 tells us that the king of Egypt died. We refer to him as the pharaoh of the oppression; his successor is called the pharaoh of the Exodus. The new pharaoh continued the policy of oppressing the Israelites.

As a result, the people "sighed" and "cried out." "Sighed" means deeply sighed. "Cried out" can refer to cries to God as prayers or simply to cries of anguish. The word *groaning* in verse 24 further describes their cries. The word *cries out* is often followed by the words *unto the* LORD (Judg. 6:6–7), making clear that their cries were prayers. Very likely, some Israelites cried out in prayer and others simply cried out. In either case, "their cry came up unto God."

2. God's response (2:24–25)

> 24 And God heard their groaning, and God remembered his covenant with Abraham, with Isaac, and with Jacob.
>
> 25 And God looked upon the children of Israel, and God had respect unto them.

Four words describe God's response:

- *Heard* in the Bible means not just listening but also acting on what is heard (see Ps. 40:1–3).
- *Remembered* means not only to recall but also to act in light of that recollection. God had made a covenant with Abraham, which He renewed with Isaac and Jacob. All of Jacob or Israel's descendants were to inherit the promised land and to be God's special people. The children of Israel seemed to have forgotten that promise during the years of slavery in Egypt, but God was now about to act on it.
- *Looked upon* tells us that God saw them with compassion that led to action.
- *Had respect unto* literally means "know." God knew them in a personal and caring way.

II. The Lord Confronts Pharaoh (Exod. 5:1–2)

1. The Lord's demand (5:1)

> 1 And afterward Moses and Aaron went in, and told Pharaoh, Thus saith the LORD God of Israel, Let my people go, that they may hold a feast unto me in the wilderness.

The first clause points back to events recorded in Exodus 3–4. Exodus 5:1–2 records the opening confrontation in a contest between the Lord and Pharaoh. Speaking on behalf of "the LORD God of Israel," Moses and Aaron demanded that Pharaoh let the Lord's people go.

The word *feast* means a pilgrimage feast, or a feast at the end of a long pilgrimage. Thus, God was demanding not just a temporary release but a permanent liberation of His people.

2. Pharaoh's defiance (5:2)

> 2 And Pharaoh said, Who is the LORD, that I should obey his voice to let Israel go? I know not the LORD, neither will I let Israel go.

September 13 1998

The English words *the LORD* refer to the personal name of the God of Israel. The Lord revealed Himself to Moses during his call to lead Israel. Moses said the people would ask Moses to tell them the name of the God who promised to deliver them. God told Moses to tell them, "The LORD, God of our fathers, the God of Abraham, the God of Isaac, and the God of Jacob, hath sent me unto you" (Exod. 3:15).

Pharaoh was one of Egypt's many gods, and he had never heard of this Israelite God. Therefore, he asked, "Who is the LORD?" He answered his own question by saying that he did not know any god by such a name; therefore, he had no intention of letting the Israelite slaves go.

Pharaoh threw down the gauntlet in a test of strength between the Lord and Pharaoh. At the end of the contest, Pharaoh would know who the Lord was; and he would eagerly obey the command to let Israel go (see 7:5, 17; 8:10; 9:29).

III. The Lord Delivers Israel (Exod. 11:1–8; 12:29–32)
1. The final plague (11:1–8; 12:29–30)

> **29 And it came to pass, that at midnight the LORD smote all the firstborn in the land of Egypt, from the firstborn of Pharaoh that sat on his throne unto the firstborn of the captive that was in the dungeon; and all the firstborn of cattle.**
>
> **30 And Pharaoh rose up in the night, he, and all his servants, and all the Egyptians; and there was a great cry in Egypt; for there was not a house where there was not one dead.**

Three different words describe the miracles of deliverance that the Lord used in chapters 7–11: Signs (10:1–2), wonders (7:3; 11:9), plagues (9:14; 11:1).

- *Signs* (10:1–2) pointed to the Lord's power over the gods of Egypt.
- *Wonders* (7:3; 11:9) emphasized the wondrous effect of these miracles.
- *Plagues* in 9:14 and *plague* in 11:1 are different Hebrew words, but both words come from terms that mean to "strike" or "smite." Thus, a plague was a blow struck by the Lord. Notice the words translated "smite" or "smote" in Exodus 12:12, 13, 23, 27, 29. The Lord smote the Egyptians, the land of Egypt, and the firstborn; He did not smite the Israelites.

Ten plagues were sent against Egypt. Nine of these are recorded in Exodus 7–10. These plagues were directed against Pharaoh and the other gods of Egypt. The Egyptians worshiped things like the Nile River, the sun, and various animals. The plagues showed God's power over all these. During and after the plagues, Pharaoh alternately softened and hardened his heart. After the ninth plague, the Lord announced the final and most drastic plague (11:1–8). Earlier the Lord had told Moses to tell Pharaoh: "Israel is my son, even my firstborn. . . Let my son go, that he may serve me: and if thou refuse to let him go, behold, I will slay thy son, even thy firstborn" (Exod. 4:22–23).

Exodus 12:29–30 describes the death of the firstborn and its immediate impact on Egypt. This was the ultimate blow against the gods of Egypt. Pharaoh as a god was supposed to have some power over death, but the Lord killed not only his son but also the firstborn of all in the land. The firstborn of Pharaoh, of course, was heir to Pharoah's throne and his title as a god.

2. Pharaoh's reaction (12:31–32)

> 31 And he called for Moses and Aaron by night, and said, Rise up, and get you forth from among my people, both ye and the children of Israel; and go, serve the LORD, as ye have said.
>
> 32 Also take your flocks and your herds, as ye have said, and be gone; and bless me also.

What a striking contrast to Pharaoh's proud defiance in 5:1–2! Pharaoh had learned who the Lord was, and he was eager now to obey the Lord. He didn't wait until morning to summon Moses and Aaron; he called for them that night. Notice the dramatic effect of the words Pharaoh used in telling them to get out of Egypt.

Notice also the words "as ye have said." After one of the plagues, Pharaoh offered to let the men go but not the women and children; however, the Lord through Moses demanded that they all be set free (10:8–11). Still later, Pharaoh offered to let the people go, but not their flocks and herds; however, the Lord insisted that the people be allowed to take their livestock (10:24–26). After the final plague, Pharaoh was willing to obey fully what the Lord had demanded from the beginning.

Notice also that Pharaoh said, "And bless me also." Jacob had blessed a friendly Pharaoh of an earlier generation (Gen. 47:10). When He called Abraham, God said that Abraham would be a channel of blessings to all people (Gen. 12:1–3). Now this ruthless Pharoah, who had been humbled by the blows of the Lord, asked Moses and Aaron to bless him.

IV. Israel Celebrates Deliverance (Exod. 15:1–2, 19–21)

1. Deliverance at the Red Sea (15:19)

After the Israelites left, Exodus 14 tells how Pharaoh again hardened his heart. He sent his army after the Israelites, who found themselves trapped between the Pharoah's army and the Red Sea. The Lord sent a pillar of cloud to darken the way of the pursuing army and to shed light on His people. Then as Moses extended his rod, the Lord parted the waters of the sea until His people safely passed over. When the Egyptians pursued them, they perished in the returning waters.

2. Israel praises the Lord (15:1–2, 20–21)

> 1 Then sang Moses and the children of Israel this song unto the LORD, and spake, saying, I will sing unto the LORD, for he hath triumphed gloriously: the horse and his rider hath he thrown into the sea.

2 The LORD is my strength and song, and he is become my salvation: he is my God, and I will prepare him an habitation; my father's God, and I will exalt him.

September 13 1998

Praise is the purest language of faith. After being saved at the Red Sea, Moses and Miriam led the people in the refrain of 15:1 and 21. "Triumphed gloriously" were words that magnified the glory of the Lord and the greatness of His deliverance. "Prepare him an habitation" means to "beautify." This was a way of declaring their praise of the Lord. It goes well with the word *exalt*.

The Lord's deliverance of the Israelites from Egypt and at the Red Sea revealed His call for them to be His people. Verse 2 refers not only to Him as "my father's God" but also as "my God." The Lord is also called "my strength and song" and "my salvation." The word "my" emphasized their personal faith and praise of the Lord. They no longer worshiped Him as just the God of their forefathers, but they had also embraced Him as their God.

One message is clear through all these passages. The deliverance of Israel was God's work, not an escape engineered by Moses and the people. The people were hopeless slaves controlled and exploited by the most powerful nation on earth and the mightiest ruler. The man God called to be their human leader tried to get out of this calling. In a sense, both Moses and the Israelites were dragged kicking and screaming from their plight. Only the Lord was able to overcome Pharaoh and to lead these helpless people and their reluctant leader from Pharaoh's grasp.

SUMMARY OF BIBLE TRUTHS

1. The Lord hears the cries of His distressed people.
2. Some people openly defy the Lord.
3. God has sovereign power over all earthly powers.
4. God's deliverances are by His power, not ours.

APPLYING THE BIBLE

1. A boy was on a train, seated by himself. A man engaged him in a conversation that went something like this:

"How far are you traveling?"

"To the terminus."

"Aren't you afraid of taking such a long journey all by yourself?"

"No, sir."

"Why not?"

"Because my dad's the engineer."

Yes, we're heading to the terminus, but our Father is the engineer, as the Hebrews found out in the Exodus. "Lo, I am with you alway, even to the end of the world" (Matt. 28:20b).

2. Never alone. All of us have heard the words to this song:

You gotta walk that lonesome valley,
You gotta walk it by yourself,
Ain't nobody else can walk it for you,
You gotta walk it by yourself.

September 13 1998

But is that true? Isn't God with us all the way? You could never have convinced a thoughtful Hebrew in Moses' day, or a thoughtful Christian today, that those words have anything to do with reality!

3. God rules over all earthly powers. Exodus 12:12 says that the ten plagues were all judgments against the gods of Egypt. The plagues showed the Egyptians' gods were powerless to defend their land, and therefore worthless. The Egyptians worshiped their gods in the forms of many animals and in the person of the pharoah himself, but the plagues struck down all of these. All other gods are trivial, but our God is transcendent.

4. Lonely. Judy Garland once asked, "If I am such a legend, why am I so lonely?" Legend or not, we all feel as did Miss Garland and the Hebrews—very much alone. But to feel lonely is not to be alone!

5. God hears His people. Vincent van Gogh said, "It always strikes me, and it is very peculiar, that, whenever we see the image of indescribable and unutterable desolation—of loneliness, poverty, and misery, the end and extreme of things—the thought of God comes into our mind." But why not! "Man's extremeties are God's opportunities." And, "My disappointments are God's appointments." And, "One can see further (even to heaven!) through tears than through a telescope."

6. What will you do with your freedom? Listen to how one man handled his freedom: "He is much more than the George Washington of South America. He is the Washington, the Patrick Henry, the Thomas Jefferson, the Abraham Lincoln. He initiated the revolution against Spain which gave five nations birth; he commanded the armies which won their freedom; he formulated the principles upon which the republics were founded, formed their governments, and wrote their constitutions. . . . To many millions of South Americans today, (this man) is almost a deity. Far more than any figure in English or North American history, (he) exists in the consciousness of his people as a living entity." But at one point he was "a penniless exile on the island of Curacao. . . . Everything he owned—his great estates, vast herds of cattle, blocks of city property—was gone, confiscated by the Spaniards. He had to beg from strangers to keep himself alive." He escaped prison and his first command was two hundred men. But from that, Simon Bolivar rose to immense fame. He made good use of his freedom in seeking it, passionately, for others![1]

7. Praise ever must be the response to all God has done for us! "Good heaven! Any one thing in the creation is sufficient to demonstrate a Providence to a humble and grateful mind. The mere possibility of producing milk from grass, cheese from milk, and wool from skins; who formed and planned it? Ought we not, whether we dig or plough or eat, to sing this hymn to God? Great is God, who has supplied us with these instruments to till the ground; who has given us to grow insensibly and to breathe in sleep. These things we ought forever to celebrate. . . . But because the most of you are blind and insensible, there must be someone to fill this station, and lead, in behalf of all men, the hymn to God. Were I a nightingale, I would act the part of a nightingale; were I a swan, the part of a swan. But since I am a reasonable creature, it is my duty to praise God . . . and I call on you to join the same song." And all that from a pagan! If, according to him, reason alone produced such profound praise to God, how much more revelation!"[2]

September 13 1998

TEACHING THE BIBLE

▸ *Main Idea:* The Exodus was a divine deliverance, not a human escape.

▸ *Suggested Teaching Aim:* To lead adults to identify ways God can deliver them from whatever would enslave them.

A TEACHING OUTLINE

God Delivers a People from Slavery

1. God Remembers His Covenant (Exod. 2:23–25).
2. The Lord Confronts Pharaoh (Exod. 5:1–2).
3. The Lord Delivers Israel (Exod. 11:1–8; 12:29–32).
4. Israel Celebrates Deliverance (Exod. 15:1–2, 19–21).

Introduce the Bible Study

Ask members to mention various forces that can enslave people. (Physical slavery, drugs, work, etc.) Point out that our lesson for today describes how God delivered the Israelites from physical slavery and that He is still in the business of delivering people from whatever enslaves them.

Search for Biblical Truth

Enlist two members to read alternately the eight summary statements in "Outline and Summary" to overview the lesson.

On a chalkboard make the following chart:

Important Words

Verse	Words	Meaning
2:23	"sighed"	
	"cried"	
2:24	"groaning"	
2:24	"heard"	
	"remembered"	
2:25	"looked upon"	
	"had respect unto"	
5:1	"feast"	
5:2	"the LORD"	
7:3	"wonders"	
10:1–2	"signs"	
11:1	"plague"	

PAGE 17

September 13, 1998

Important Words

Verse	Words	Meaning
12:32	"bless me"	
15:1	"triumphed gloriously"	
15:2	"my strength and song . . ."	
	salvation . . . God . . . father's	
	"God"	

Ask someone to read 2:23–25. Point out the three words that describe Israel's reaction. (Sighed, cried, groaning.) Write the meaning of the words given in "Studying the Bible" on the chart.

Point out the four words that describe God's response (heard, remembered, looked upon, had respect unto) and write the meanings on the chart.

Ask someone to read 5:1–2. Explain "Feast" and "the LORD" and write the meanings on the chart.

Ask someone to read 11:1–8; 12:29–32 as well as 10:1–2; 7:3; 9:14. Explain "signs," "wonders," "plagues," "as ye said," and "bless me also" and write the meanings on the chart.

Ask someone to read 15:1–2, 20–21 and explain "triumphed gloriously," "prepare him an habitation," and "my strength and song . . . salvation . . . God . . . father's God" and write the meanings on the chart.

Share the four statements in the "Summary of Bible Truths" and suggest that these are lessons that still apply to us today.

Give the Truth a Personal Focus

Ask, What evidence do you see that this deliverance from Egypt was not just something human but something divine? List these reasons on a chalkboard.

Ask, What evidence do you see that God can still deliver people from their slavery today?

Challenge members to claim God's strength and deliverance from whatever force has them enslaved.

---

1. The quotes are from *Great Lives, Great Deeds* (Pleasantville, N.Y.: Reader's Digest Association, 1964), 214, 217.

2. The quote is from William James, *Varieties of Religious Experience* (1858); reprint edition (New York: Mentor Books), p. 359.

What God Expects

Background Passage: Deuteronomy 5:1–21
Focal Passages: Deuteronomy 5:6–14a, 16–21

September
20
1998

The Ten Commandments were the heart of what God expected of Israel as He entered into covenant with them. The Ten Commandments appear twice: once in Exodus 20:1–17 when God made the covenant and again in Deuteronomy 5:6–21 as the next generation prepared to enter Canaan. This repetition underscores their importance.

▶**Study Aim:** *To name and briefly explain each of the Ten Commandments.*

STUDYING THE BIBLE

OUTLINE AND SUMMARY

I. Our Relationship with God (Deut. 5:1–15)
   1. First Commandment (5:1–7)
   2. Second Commandment (5:8–10)
   3. Third Commandment (5:11)
   4. Fourth Commandment (5:12–16)

II. Our Relationship with Others (Deut. 5:16–21)
   1. Fifth Commandment (5:16)
   2. Sixth Commandment (5:17)
   3. Seventh Commandment (5:18)
   4. Eighth Commandment (5:19)
   5. Ninth Commandment (5:20)
   6. Tenth Commandment (5:21)

The first commandment demands that we worship only the Lord God (5:1–7). The second condemns worship that uses images (5:8–10). The third condemns manipulating, belittling, or distorting God (5:11). The fourth commands honoring God by refraining from work on the Sabbath day (5:12–16). The fifth commands respect for parents (5:16). The sixth condemns murder (5:17); the seventh, adultery (5:18); the eighth, stealing (5:19); the ninth, telling lies about others (5:20); and the tenth, coveting what belongs to someone else (5:21).

I. Our Relationship with God (Deut. 5:1–15)

1. First Commandment (Deut. 5:1–7)

> 6 I am the LORD thy God, which brought thee out of the land of Egypt, from the house of bondage.
>
> 7 Thou shalt have none other gods before me.

Moses emphasized that the Ten Commandments were given not only to those who first heard them but also to succeeding generations of His people (5:1–5). Based on the Lord's deliverance of Israel from Egypt (5:6), God called Israel to be His people and to obey His Commandments (Exod. 19:1–20:17).

September 20, 1998

The first four commandments have to do with people's relation with God, and the last six have to do with relations with others. Unless our relation with God is right, we have little hope of right relations with other people. The first commandment calls for exclusive worship of the Lord. This was crucial in a world in which people worshiped many gods. Worshipers of many gods had to spread their devotion among their gods. Those who worship only the Lord are expected to give Him total devotion and love (Deut. 6:4–5).

2. Second Commandment (5:8–10)

8 Thou shalt not make thee any graven image, or any likeness of any thing that is in heaven above, or that is in the earth beneath, or that is in the waters beneath the earth:

9 Thou shalt not bow down thyself unto them, nor serve them: for I the LORD thy God am a jealous God, visiting the iniquity of the fathers upon the children unto the third and fourth generation of them that hate me,

10 And shewing mercy unto thousands of them that love me and keep my commandments.

We may think that the second commandment only repeats the first, because the worship of false gods usually involved images. However, some Israelites tried to worship God with images. God reveals Himself as He chooses; but when people make images, they make the decision of what God is like. These human creations distort what God is like. Images also enable the image maker to manipulate what he has made, but God is beyond human control.

This commandment is accompanied with a warning and a promise. God will judge those who show their disdain by breaking His commandments, but He extends mercy freely to those who love Him and keep His commandments.

3. Third Commandment (5:11)

11 Thou shalt not take the name of the LORD thy God in vain: for the LORD will not hold him guiltless that taketh his name in vain.

The name of God represents the character of God. This commandment condemns blasphemy and swearing. People also take God's name in vain when they go through the motions of meaningless praying or worshiping. Ancient people believed that if people knew the name of a god, they could exercise some control over the god by using the god's name to get what they wanted. The third commandment is directed against any such attempt to manipulate the Lord.

4. Fourth Commandment (5:12–16)

12 Keep the sabbath day to sanctify it, as the LORD thy God hath commanded thee.

13 Six days thou shalt labour, and do all thy work:

14 But the seventh day is the sabbath of the LORD thy God: in it thou shalt not do any work.

September 20, 1998

Setting aside the Sabbath day was a way of dedicating all days to God. In other words, the person who kept the Sabbath day for rest, meditation, and worship also committed the other six days to work and other daily activities in the name of the Lord.

The reason for this commandment in Exodus 20:11 is that the Lord created all things in six days and rested on the seventh day. The reason given in Deuteronomy 5:14b–15 is that the Lord delivered Israel from ceaseless toil in Egyptian slavery. These two reasons complement, not contradict, each other. That is, one purpose of setting aside one day is that this conforms to the nature of God, in whose image we are made. God works, but He also rests. Life's cycles include time for both work and rest. Also the fourth commandment freed the Israelites from a life of ceaseless toil. By divine commandment, slave owners, parents, and employers were commanded to provide time for rest.

II. Our Relationship with Others (Deut. 5:16–21)
1. Fifth Commandment (5:16)

> **16 Honour thy father and thy mother, as the LORD thy God hath commanded thee; that thy days may be prolonged, and that it may go well with thee, in the land which the LORD thy God giveth thee.**

The fifth commandment and the seventh commandment protect the family, the basic building block of human society. God ordained marriage and parenthood as part of His good creation. Thus, it was appropriate to introduce the six commandments about human relations by commanding honor to parents. The promise attached to the fifth commandment means that human well-being is dependent on maintaining the integrity of the family. When families deteriorate, the foundation of human society is eroded. When families are healthy, everything else can build on a strong foundation.

This commandment means that children who are still under their parents' roof must obey (Eph. 6:1). When children grow up and establish their own homes (Gen. 2:24), they are still to honor and respect their parents. This not only provides stability for society but also ensures that the heritage of faith will be passed on from one generation to the next.

2. Sixth Commandment (5:17)

> **17 Thou shalt not kill.**

The sixth commandment was designed to protect human life. Human life has value because human beings are created in the image of God (Gen. 9:6). This commandment referred only to murder in the day it was given. It did not forbid taking life in war or legitimate courts enforcing capital punishment.

Christians, of course, are still bound by the basic moral and spiritual standards of the Ten Commandments. In fact, the New Testament expects far more of us than that we not murder others. Jesus taught that the inner attitudes of hatred and the deadly power of abusive words also break the spirit of this commandment (Matt. 5:21–22).

Jesus and the apostles also taught that we are bound by the demands of love—for God and for others. "Love thy neighbour as thyself" fulfills the sixth and other commandments about human relations (Rom. 13:9). The commandments against murder, adultery, stealing, and bearing false witness merely set the minimum standard below which people of faith will not sink. Love demands much more. For example, love demands that we return good for evil instead of evil for evil (Rom. 12:19–21).

3. Seventh Commandment (5:18)

18 Neither shalt thou commit adultery.

This commandment protects the sanctity of marriage. The family is the basic building block of society, and marriage is the basic relation in a family. When God instituted marriage, He said that marriage was to be a one-flesh union of husband and wife (Gen. 2:24). Jesus made clear that this relationship is to be exclusive and to last a lifetime (Matt. 19:3–6). Such a relationship demands complete trust in each other and faithfulness to each other.

Sex fulfills its purpose in the one-flesh union of husband and wife. Using sex outside of this divine intention violates this commandment. Sexual immorality is such a deadly sin because so many people are hurt by it. Sometimes a person will say: "I know what I'm doing is wrong, but I'm hurting no one but myself." This is never true of the sin of adultery.

4. The Eighth Commandment (5:19)

19 Neither shalt thou steal.

This commandment protects a person's right to have something of his own. One purpose of Christian work is to have something to give to the needy (Eph. 4:28). If you owned nothing, you would have nothing to care for your own needs or to help others. You would be dependent on someone else. You would have no freedom of action.

Thus, when someone steals another person's possessions, the thief is taking more than money or property; the thief is taking the victim's ability to feed his family, to provide education and medical care, and to give to missions and to needy people. No wonder that victims of robbery feel violated—as if they have lost some of their dignity, freedom, and value as persons.

Name all the words that describe various forms of taking what belongs to someone else. Don't forget words like *pilfer, extort, swindle, defraud, cheat*. The list will be longer than you think. It will remind you that many people break this commandment in ways other than robbery and theft. The fact that we need so many words to describe this sin shows how widespread it is.

5. Ninth Commandment (5:20)

20 Neither shalt thou bear false witness against thy neighbour.

This commandment is designed to protect a person's reputation and good name. The most direct application of this commandment is lying about someone in a court of law. However, the most frequent violators of the ninth commandment are people who spread gossip filled with lies, half-truths, and rumors about other people.

Human relations are built on honesty and trust. If someone speaks or acts contrary to the truth, how can anyone trust anything this person says? This is true in the family, the community, in business, and in any kind of relationship.

6. Tenth Commandment (5:21)

> 21 Neither shalt thou desire thy neighbour's wife, neither shalt thou covet thy neighbor's house, his field, or his manservant, or his maidservant, his ox, or his ass, or any thing that is thy neighbour's.

The tenth commandment differs from the others because it focuses on an attitude rather than an action. By focusing on the sinful attitude that lies behind sinful action, the tenth commandment anticipated what Jesus taught in Matthew 5:21–22, 27–28. Covetousness often leads to breaking the other commandments. First Kings 21:1–17 tells how Ahab coveted Naboth's [NAY bahth] vineyard. Jezebel got it for him by bribing witnesses against Naboth (ninth commandment), having Naboth and his family unjustly put to death (sixth), and confiscating Naboth's vineyard (eighth). Second Samuel 11 tells how David coveted Uriah's [yoo RIGH uh] wife. After committing adultery with her (seventh), he tried to cover up his sin by issuing an order that resulted in Uriah's death (sixth).

SUMMARY OF BIBLE TRUTHS

1. A right relation with God is the foundation for right relations with other people.
2. A right relation with God involves putting Him first, worshiping Him as He has revealed Himself, respecting His name, and keeping the Sabbath Day.
3. Right relations with others begins with right relations within the family.
4. Commandments six through nine protect human life, marriage, property, and reputation.
5. Covetousness can lead to breaking the other commandments.

APPLYING THE BIBLE

1. The Ten Commandments. News commentator Ted Koppel once did a piece on the Ten Commandments. He said they are not ten suggestions but the Ten Commandments and that wise men will accede to that.

2. Responding to what God has done for us. Our key verse teaches that God's call for us to obey is based on His previous redemptive act of delivering and redeeming us. It is not "payback" time, but it is R&R time—remembrance and response time!

3. Breaking the law. All meaningful life honors law. In every realm. It realizes that no one ever breaks a law; he only violates it, and in doing so, demonstrates it. The law is not broken; he is. If one jumps off a high building, he does not break the law of gravity, but, rather, proves it. So, nobody's "getting by with it."

4. Two tables of the law. The Ten Commandments are divided into "two tables," as older theologians called them. That is to say, some of the commandments deal with our relationship to God (the "vertical" emphasis) and the other with our relationship to other people (the "horizontal"

September 20, 1998

emphasis). The Ten Commandments teach us first to obey God and then to serve others. This is shocking to modern man. A right relation with God is the foundation for right relations with other people.

5. Putting God last. A university ethics professor asked students to rearrange the Ten Commandments to make them more suitable in a modern world. Most of the students reversed numbers one and ten. Avoiding covetousness became the first priority and putting God first fell to the bottom of the list!

6. Expecting more from God than from ourselves. Isn't it amazing how keen we are about God doing the right thing in all circumstances, even though we respond in a very cavalier way to His commands? If God should be responsible, why shouldn't we?

7. Responsibility and irresponsibility. Henry Kissinger once said, "If you think responsibility is hard to bear, you should try irresponsibility." How is irresponsibility hard to bear?

8. Obedient action. All blessing comes from obeying God. According to C. S. Lewis, the devil reasons along these lines: "As long as [the new Christian] does not convert [an idea God has given him] into action, it does not matter how much he thinks about this new repentance. Let the little brute wallow in it. Let him, if he has any bent that way, write a book about it; that is often an excellent way of sterilizing the seeds which the Enemy plants in a human soul. Let him do anything but act. No amount of piety in his imagination and affections will harm us if we can keep it out of his will. As one of the humans has said, active habits are strengthened by repetition but passive ones are weakened. The more often he feels without acting, the less he will be able ever to act, and, in the long run, the less he will be able to feel."[1]

9. Doing the truth, not just knowing the truth. If preaching could save America, we would have been saved a dozen times in the last month! If reading Christian books would do it, again, we would have been saved several times over this year! If knowing truth could produce Utopia, the perfect society, we could let all the police officers and attorneys and judges go fishing! Permanently!

10. On the light side.

- Forbidden fruit is responsible for many bad jams.
- "It was not the apple on the tree, but the pair on the ground that caused the trouble in the garden" (M. D. O'Connor).
- "Sometimes a nation abolishes God; fortunately, God is more tolerant."

11. Think on these things.

- If your only praise to God, as a Christian, occurred during formal worship sessions, would that be a sufficient expression of love to Him?
- How else, and in what settings, should we praise God?
- Do those who know you best see that praise is a key element in your life?
- Why are many Christians inhibited in their praise of God?

TEACHING THE BIBLE

September 20 1998

▸ *Main Idea:* God gave Ten Commandments to tell Israel and us how He expects us to live.
▸ *Suggested Teaching Aim:* To lead adults to identify ways the Ten Commandments are still relevant today.

A TEACHING OUTLINE

What God Expects

I. Our Relationship with God (Deut. 5:1–15)
   1. First Commandment (5:1–7)
   2. Second Commandment (5:8–10)
   3. Third Commandment (5:11)
   4. Fourth Commandment (5:12–16)
II. Our Relationship with Others (Deut. 5:16–21)
   1. Fifth Commandment (5:16)
   2. Sixth Commandment (5:17)
   3. Seventh Commandment (5:18)
   4. Eighth Commandment (5:19)
   5. Ninth Commandment (5:20)
   6. Tenth Commandment (5:21)

Introduce the Bible Study

IN ADVANCE, make a large poster with the words: "I am the Lord thy God: Therefore . . ." and place it on the focal wall. Make ten posters with numbers 1–10 on them and place them in order beneath the above poster. Make ten other posters with brief summaries of each of the Ten Commandments on them (number these with small numbers only you can see if you need help); place these at random on the wall. Ask members to arrange these in the proper order. Ask them to think why God may have chosen this order.

Search for Biblical Truth

IN ADVANCE, make the "Teaching Outline" poster and use it to show the two divisions of the commandments. **IN ADVANCE**, cut an 8 1/2-by-11-inch sheet of paper into ten strips. In large letters, label the strips "First Commandment," "Second Commandment," and so on. Place a piece of tape on the end of each strip and tape the strips to a wall in order.

For each of the commandments, use the following procedure:
(1) Ask someone to read the Scripture passage from Deuteronomy.
(2) Ask, What did this Commandment mean to ancient Israel?
(3) Ask, How did ancient Israel violate this commandment?
(4) Ask, How do we violate this commandment today?
(5) Ask, How is this commandment relevant today?
(6) Remove the appropriate strip from the wall and tape the ends together, forming a link in a chain. Tape the first link to the wall.

September 20, 1998

After the first link, tape all links together to form a chain. When you put up the tenth link, tape that link to the wall as well so the chain hangs suspended by the first and tenth links.

As an alternate procedure, if your class works well in small groups, you might assign one or two of the commandments to each group and let them answer the questions and make the chain.

Share the five "Summary of Bible Truths" statements.

Give the Truth a Personal Focus

Read "Putting God last" from "Applying the Bible." Ask members to defend the current order of the Ten Commandments. Why is it best?

Refer to the chain representing the Ten Commandments. Ask: Which one is most important? What happens if we break even one? Take a pair of scissors and cut any one of the links. Ask, What happens when we break one of the commandments? The New Testament says that if we break one commandment, we are guilty of breaking them all (James. 2:10). If we are depending on the commandments to get us into heaven, it doesn't make any difference which one we break; the chain will let us fall. We need to know God's grace and forgiveness to make up for our failure.

---

1. C. S. Lewis, *The Screwtape Letters* (New York: Bantam Books, 1982), 390.

Remembering What God Has Done

September 27 1998

Background Passage: Joshua 3:7–4:24
Focal Passages: Joshua 4:1–3, 8, 10–11, 20–24

Since this quarter is a survey of the Old Testament, we need to stop occasionally to overview what we have covered. The period of beginnings, found in Genesis 1–11, extends from the creation to the time of Abraham. The period of the patriarchs, found in Genesis 12–50, covers from Abraham through Joseph. The period of the Exodus, found in the books of Exodus, Leviticus, Numbers, and Deuteronomy, begins with the deliverance from Egypt and concludes with the Israelites ready to enter the promised land. The period of the Conquest, found in Joshua, tells of Israel's crossing the Jordan until the death of Joshua.

▶**Study Aim:** *To explain the purposes of the memorial of twelve stones.*

STUDYING THE BIBLE

OUTLINE AND SUMMARY
  I. **Crossing the Jordan River (Josh. 3:7–4:18)**
     1. **Preparing for crossing (3:7–13)**
     2. **Stopping the waters (3:14–17)**
     3. **Gathering twelve stones (4:1–9)**
     4. **Completing the crossing (4:10–18)**
  II. **Establishing a Memorial (Josh. 4:19–24)**
     1. **Building a memorial (4:19–20)**
     2. **Creating a teaching opportunity (4:21–22)**
     3. **Testifying to what the Lord did (4:23)**
     4. **Knowing God's power and fearing Him (4:24)**

The Lord gave instructions about crossing the Jordan River (3:7–13). When the priests and people obeyed, the Lord stopped the waters of the flooded Jordan (3:14–17). The Lord commanded that twelve stones be taken from the riverbed (4:1–9). After the people and priests had crossed over, the waters returned (4:10–18). The twelve stones were set up at Gilgal (4:19–20). These stones became a teaching opportunity for future generations (4:21–22). The stones testified of the Lord's parting of the Jordan (4:23). This fact should cause the pagans to know the Lord's mighty power and to inspire the Israelites to fear the Lord forever (4:24).

I. Crossing the Jordan River (Josh. 3:7–4:18)
1. Preparing for crossing (3:7–13)
Moses had been the human leader during the deliverance, the making of the covenant, and the years in the wilderness. Now Moses was dead, and God had anointed Joshua to be the human leader during the conquest of Canaan. God told Joshua that He would reinforce Joshua as leader by

the manner of crossing the Jordan River (3:7–8). Joshua told the people that God would give them a reassuring sign that He would drive out all the people now in Canaan (3:9–10). Joshua promised that the Lord Himself, whose presence was signified by the ark of the covenant, would go before them (3:11). When the feet of the priests carrying the ark touched the Jordan River, the waters would be stopped (3:13).

2. Stopping the waters (3:14–17)

The people and priests obeyed the Lord's command through Joshua. The priests led the way into the swollen river. The river was swollen because it was the spring of the year when the waters were at flood stage (3:14–15). When the priests entered the river, "the waters which came down from above stood and rose up upon an heap" (3:16). The waters that flowed down from the north "were cut off," enabling the people to cross near the city of Jericho (3:16). The priests bearing the ark marched to the center of the riverbed and "stood firm on dry ground in the midst of Jordan, and all the Israelites passed over on dry ground, until all the people were passed clean over Jordan" (3:17). This miracle was obviously done by the Lord, not by Joshua or the priests.

3. Gathering twelve stones (4:1–9)

> 1 And it came to pass, when all the people were clean passed over Jordan, that the LORD spake unto Joshua saying,
>
> 2 Take you twelve men out of the people, out of every tribe a man,
>
> 3 And command ye them, saying, Take you hence out of the midst of the Jordan, out of the place where the priests' feet stood firm, twelve stones, and ye shall carry them over with you, and leave them in the lodging place, where ye shall lodge this night.

Earlier, according to 3:12, the Lord had told Joshua to select twelve men, one from each tribe. These likely were the same men mentioned in 4:1–3. Each man was instructed to pick up a stone from the riverbed, where the priests stood. Each was told to carry the stone with him and to leave it at the place where they camped that night. Joshua explained that this heap of stones would serve as a reminder to them and to future generations of what the Lord had done in stopping the waters of the Jordan River to allow the Israelites to enter the promised land (4:4–7).

> 8 And the children of Israel did so as Joshua commanded, and took up twelve stones out of the midst of Jordan, as the LORD spake unto Joshua, according to the number of the tribes of the children of Israel, and carried them over with them unto the place where they lodged, and laid them down there.

Verse 8 shows how carefully and fully the people obeyed the command of the Lord as communicated to them through their new leader. This shows their obedience to God and their recognition of Joshua as their leader.

Verse 9 mentions placing twelve stones in the midst of the river. Apparently, the twelve men brought stones from the east bank and made a pile to commemorate the place where the priests had stood.

4. Completing the crossing (4:10–18)

> **10 For the priests which bare the ark stood in the midst of Jordan, until every thing was finished that the LORD commanded Joshua to speak unto the people, according to all that Moses commanded Joshua: and the people hasted and passed over.**
>
> **11 And it came to pass, when all the people were clean passed over, that the ark of the LORD passed over, and the priests, in the presence of the people.**

Throughout this event, the priests acted with amazing faith and complete obedience. Notice that the waters did not part before the feet of the priests touched the water, but only after they actually marched into the water. After reaching the center of the riverbed, they stood holding the ark while all the people passed through the riverbed to the other side. Only after everyone was safely across did the priests leave their place and go to the other side.

The people themselves are said to have "hasted and passed over." This does not necessarily imply that they lacked faith that God would continue to stop the waters, but it shows that they wisely wasted no time.

Verse 11 emphasizes that the ark of the Lord passed over after all the people (from all twelve tribes, 4:12–13) were safely across. His presence, signified by the ark, was what held back the waters. The words "in the presence of the people" can mean either that the ark was seen by all the people or that the ark was taken to its place in front of the people as they moved forward.

The effect of this miracle was as the Lord had predicted. The people magnified Joshua as their new leader and showed him the kind of fear and respect they had shown Moses (4:14). It was Joshua who told the priests when to complete their crossing. As soon as they were across, the waters of the river returned and overflowed the river banks (4:15–18).

II. Establishing a Memorial (Josh. 4:19–24)

1. Building a memorial (4:19–20)

> **20 And those twelve stones, which they took out of Jordan, did Joshua pitch in Gilgal.**

Israel camped that night at Gilgal [GIL gal], located between the Jordan River and Jericho [JER ih koh]. There Joshua set up the twelve stones as the Lord had commanded (4:8). When Abraham first entered Canaan, he built an altar and worshiped the Lord (Gen. 12:8). On their first night there, the Israelites followed the example of Abraham.

Gilgal became the base camp for the attack on Jericho, the next major obstacle to conquering the land. The people celebrated their first Passover in Canaan at Gilgal (5:11–12). The Lord spoke to Joshua and reassured him of victory (5:13–15). Gilgal continued to provide a base from which the Conquest continued after Jericho fell (Josh. 9:6; 10:6; 14:6). The emphasis in Joshua 4:20, however, is on the memorial of twelve

September 27, 1998

stones at Gilgal. On more than one occasion, a stone or stones were used to mark significant events (see Gen. 28:10–22; 31:25–52; 1 Sam. 7:12).

2. Creating a teaching opportunity (4:21–22)

> **21 And he spake unto the children of Israel, saying, When your children shall ask their fathers in time to come, saying, What mean these stones?**
>
> **22 Then ye shall let your children know, saying, Israel came over this Jordan on dry land.**

A primary purpose of the memorial was to ensure that the faith of Israel was communicated from generation to generation. The stones provided a teaching opportunity for parents. When children saw the stones, they would ask what they meant. Then the parents would tell how the Lord delivered Israel from Egypt by parting the Red Sea and opened the way into the promised land by parting the Jordan River.

Joshua 4:21 is similar to Exodus 12:26 and Deuteronomy 6:20. All three passages tell of practices designed to create interest and curiosity in children. As a Hebrew family observed the Passover, small children would ask why they did that and what it meant. Then parents would tell them of the Lord's deliverance of their forefathers from Egyptian slavery through the death of the firstborn. Likewise, after reciting the *shema* (Deut. 6:4–5), parents were to teach their children (Deut. 6:6–9). As parents taught their children God's commandments, the children would ask their meaning. Parents would then testify to God's mighty deeds in delivering His people (Deut. 6:20–25).

Three facts stand out:

- Remembering what God had done for Israel was crucial to Israel's distinctive faith.
- The children of Israel should pass on their faith from one generation to another.
- Parents were the primary teachers, and memorials provided a teaching opportunity by leading children to ask questions. Unlike some modern parents, Israelite parents saw questions from their children as great opportunities for teaching them the faith.

3. Testifying to what the Lord did (4:23)

> **23 For the LORD your God dried up the waters of the Jordan from before you, until ye were passed over, as the LORD your God did to the Red sea, which he dried up from before us, until we were clean gone over.**

Notice that verse 23 linked together the miracles at the Red Sea and the Jordan River. Both were important miracles of the Lord in leading His people from slavery to the promised land. Just as Moses had not parted the Red Sea by his own power, neither had Joshua or the priests parted the Jordan by their own power. The Lord had done both these miracles.

Remember is an important Bible word. As used in the Bible, the word means more than an intellectual ability to recall something. The word includes the appropriate actions called for by that memory. For example, the preface to the Ten Commandments is a reminder that the Lord who gave the commandments for them to obey was the Lord who had delivered them from Egypt (Exod. 20:2; Deut. 5:6). Remembering what God did in the past inspires present obedience and faith as we advance into the future.

4. Knowing God's power and fearing Him (4:24)

> 24 That all the people of the earth might know the hand of the LORD, that it is mighty: that ye might fear the LORD your God for ever.

Verse 24 spells out a twofold purpose for the memorial. First of all, the news of crossing the Jordan River was designed to cause the pagan nations of the earth—especially those in Canaan—to know the mighty power of the Lord. The miracle had this desired effect. When the kings of the groups in Canaan heard of the miracle, "their heart melted" (Josh. 5:1). They had expected the flooded Jordan at least to slow the relentless Israelite advance, but then they heard that the Lord parted the river. Israel was already in Canaan.

The second purpose was directed at the Israelites themselves ("ye"). This mighty sign and wonder was another reason for the Israelites to fear and trust the Lord their God.

SUMMARY OF BIBLE TRUTHS

1. Faith involves launching out in total reliance on God.
2. The fulfillment of many of God's promises is dependent on our faith.
3. Special places and events remind us of what God has done for us in the past.
4. Remembering God's past deliverances enables us to trust Him to guide and help us in the present and the future.
5. Believing parents need to pass on their faith to their children.
6. Bearing testimony to God's deliverances can be used to convict unbelievers of their need for God.

APPLYING THE BIBLE

1. Symbols. C. S. Lewis once said, "Symbols are the natural speech of the soul, a language older and more universal than words." Today's lesson is about the meaning of the symbols Israel placed as a memorial in the Jordan River upon the occasion of their crossing into the promised land. Symbols like the flag or a wedding ring evoke powerful memories. What are some of the most powerful symbols in your life?

2. Of what use is history? Henry Ford once said, "History is bunk." Perhaps he was thinking of ways we can misuse history:
- by failing to learn from it,
- by misinterpreting it,
- by appealing to it to avoid creative effort,
- by embellishing it until it becomes a lie, and
- by worshiping the symbols of the past while refusing to pursue the substance of the future.

September 27, 1998

Our Bible and our faith are based on the conviction that we can learn from the past. History is not bunk, although we may dismiss in that way.

3. Are you an Abraham? According to Hebrews 11:23–28, Moses' faith caused him to do four things:
(1) to refuse to be called the son of Pharoah's daughter,
(2) to choose to suffer with God's people instead of enjoying the pleasures of sin for a season,
(3) To forsake Egypt despite the Pharoah's displeasure, and
(4) To keep the passover.

Let's notice some important things about Abraham's four acts of faith:

- They all cost Moses dearly.
- They were all by choice.
- They demanded his continuous commitment and obedience.
- They put him in the minority—all faith activity does!
- They were all done strictly by faith and not by sight.
- They all put his life in jeopardy.

Does your faith look and act like that? Can you think of acts you have taken where those principles were manifest?

4. Heroes of faith.
Men who see the invisible,
And hear the inaudible,
Believe the incredible,
Think the unthinkable,
And do the impossible.

5. Faith in despair. The Israelites were incapable of expressing true faith until they were trapped between the wilderness on one side and the "ites" on the other—Jebusites, Canaanites, and the other "ites." Sometimes we're like the Israelites. A lot of Christians are unsure about whether God heals miraculously—until their child needs His miraculous intervention! Sometimes this experience clarifies our theology! Perhaps it can be no other way. Soren Kierkegaard once said, "For practical purposes it is at the hopeless moment that we require the hopeful man. . . . Exactly where hope ceases to be reasonable, it begins to be useful."[1]

6. Asking for a miracle. Sometimes I ask my congregation, at the time of the Sunday morning prayer, "How many of you are facing situations, right now, where you need God to come through miraculously?" Almost always, everybody raises their hands. Would you raise yours, right now, if I asked you that question? (I just did something you might want to know about: I just prayed that, whenever and wherever this lesson is taught, for all those who would so raise their hands, God would deliver—in a marvelous demonstration of His supernatural grace! You have been prayed for!)

7. Totally insured. If we never express faith in God, if we never walk by faith, if we never risk anything, then we're not really living.

There was a very cautious man,
who never laughed or cried
He never risked, he never lost,

he never won nor tried.
And when one day he passed away
his insurance was denied,
For since he never really lived
they claimed he never died!

September 27 1998

TEACHING THE BIBLE

▶ *Main Idea:* Remembering what God has done can strengthen our faith.
▶ *Suggested Teaching Aim:* To lead adults to remember what God has done so their faith may be strengthened.

A TEACHING OUTLINE

Remembering What God Has Done

1. *Crossing the Jordan River (Josh. 3:7–4:18)*
2. *Establishing a Memorial (Josh. 4:19–24)*

Introduce the Bible Study

Enlist four people to read the four statements in the introduction of this lesson to overview the quarter's study. Point out that our lesson today is entitled "Remembering What God Has Done." Ask, What one lesson can you remember from Genesis 1–11? from Genesis 12–50? from the period of the Exodus?

Search for Biblical Truth

IN ADVANCE, make six posters with the word *Remember!* on them. Post these around the room as silent teachers.

Use "Studying the Bible" to set the context of today's lesson. If you have access to a wall map, locate the Jordan River, Jericho, approximate location of Gilgal, Adam, and Zaretan (Josh. 3:16).

Ask someone to read Joshua 4:1–3, 8, 10–11. Point out the great faith required for the priests to enter the flooded river. Point out that part of the great miracle was that the water stopped at the exact time they entered the water.

Distribute paper and pencils and ask members to write a brief paragraph describing what they think they would have felt about the miracle if they had been a part of the Israelite company that day. Let all who wish read their paragraphs aloud.

Ask someone to read Joshua 4:19–24. **IN ADVANCE**, enlist a member to read "Gilgal" in *Holman Bible Dictionary* or other Bible dictionary and share a two- to three-minute report with the class. Ask, Do you remember another Old Testament character who had built an altar when he first entered Canaan? (Abraham—Gen. 12:8.) Do you remember other times stones were set up to mark significant events? (Gen. 28:10–22; 31:25–52; 1 Sam. 7:12.) What was the primary purpose of set-

September 27, 1998

ting up the twelve stones? (Ensure that the faith of Israel was communicated from generation to generation.)

Ask one person to read aloud Exodus 12:26 and another to read Deuteronomy 6:20. Ask, How are these two passages and Joshua 4:21 similar? (All tell of practices designed to create children's interest.)

Share these three facts drawn from this passage:
- Remembering what God had done for Israel was crucial to Israel's distinctive faith.
- This faith needed to be passed on from one generation to another.
- Parents were the primary teachers, and memorials provided a teaching opportunity by leading children to ask questions.

Ask members to look at 4:24 and find two purposes for the memorial. (Reminded pagan nations that Israel's God had moved them across a flooded river and reminded Israel to fear and trust God.)

Restate the six statements in "Summary of Bible Truths."

Give the Truth a Personal Focus

Ask: What event in your life would come closest to crossing the flooded Jordan? How has remembering this event helped you in difficult times? How can you build a fitting memorial to help you and others remember God's goodness and faithfulness?

Close with sentence prayers from the group thanking God for doing some particular work in their lives.

---

1. Soren Kierkegaard, *The Works of Love*, translated by David and Lillian Swenson (Princeton, N.J.: Princeton University Press, 1946), 199.

Cycle of Sin and Judgment

October 4, 1998

Background Passage: Judges 2
Focal Passage: Judges 2:11–20

We have moved through the periods of beginnings, patriarchs, exodus, and conquest. Now we come to the period of the judges. The period was characterized by a recurring cycle of sin, punishment, and deliverance. The period gets its name from the deliverers, who were called judges.

▶**Study Aim:** *To briefly describe the stages in the recurring cycle found in the book of Judges.*

STUDYING THE BIBLE

OUTLINE AND SUMMARY
I. From Obedience to Disobedience (Judg. 2:1–10)
    1. Punishment for disobedience (2:1–5)
    2. Flashback to better days (2:6–10)
II. A Deadly Cycle (Judg. 2:11–23)
    1. Sin (2:11–13)
    2. Punishment (2:14–15)
    3. Deliverance (2:16–18)
    4. Downward spiral of sin (2:19)
    5. Renewed punishment (2:20–23)

The Israelites disobeyed the Lord by failing to drive out all the pagans in Canaan (2:1–5). Those who remembered Joshua obeyed the Lord, but a later generation turned from God (2:6–10). The people forsook the Lord and committed moral evil in serving Baal (2:11–13). The Lord punished them by sending enemies who defeated and exploited the Israelites (2:14–15). The Lord responded with pity to the cries of the people and sent judges to deliver them from their enemies (2:16–18). After the judge died, the people returned to do even worse sins than before (2:19). The Lord again punished them for their sins, and so this cycle continued (2:20–23).

I. From Obedience to Disobedience (Judg. 2:1–10)
1. Punishment for disobedience (2:1–5)

The beginning of the book of Judges is closely tied to the book of Joshua. Although Joshua led in conquering the enemy armies of Canaan and distributing portions to each tribe (Josh. 11:23), individual tribes were expected to complete the conquest in their part of the land (Josh. 23:4–5). Although some of these efforts succeeded (Judg. 1:1–26), some powerful groups remained unsubdued (Judg. 1:27–33). Because the Israelites did not obey the Lord in fully destroying the inhabitants of the

October 4, 1998

land, God warned that these groups and their gods would remain as snares.

2. Flashback to better days (2:6–10)

Joshua was such an effective leader and influence that the people served the Lord during his lifetime. In fact, such was his influence that it extended beyond his death. However, a new generation arose that did not remember Joshua.

II. A Deadly Cycle (Judg. 2:11–23)

1. Sin (2:11–13)

> 11 And the children of Israel did evil in the sight of the LORD, and served Baalim:
>
> 12 And they forsook the LORD God of their fathers, which brought them out of the land of Egypt, and followed other gods, of the gods of the people that were round about them, and bowed themselves unto them, and provoked the LORD to anger.
>
> 13 And they forsook the LORD, and served Baal and Ashtaroth.

Throughout the period of the judges, the Israelites repeatedly "did evil in the sight of the LORD." The word translated "evil" refers to moral evil. Sin takes expression in various forms of moral evil, but sin is basically a spiritual problem. The reason they did evil was because "they forsook the LORD" (2:12–13). This describes the heart of what sin is. Sin is turning from the Lord, failing to trust and obey Him.

The basic expression of forsaking the Lord in Old Testament times was turning to worship other gods and to live by their pagan standards. When God made His covenant with Israel, He set forth two related expectations of them: (1) to serve the Lord only and (2) to be holy as He is holy. By contrast, pagans worshiped many gods, who made no moral demands on their worshipers. In fact, pagan religion often encouraged sinful, immoral living.

This was true of the Baal [BAY uhl] religion of the Canaanites. Baal was god of storms, rains, and vegetation. Baal worship had many local variations, but it was basically a fertility religion that promised good crops and encouraged sexual immorality as a part of its worship. The plural form of Baal, "Baalim," is sometimes used as in verse 11. Ashtaroth [ASH tuh rahth] was the plural form of Ashtoreth [ASH tuh reth], the female consort of Baal.

When the Israelites came into Canaan, they had no experience as farmers. The Canaanites were glad to tell them how to become successful farmers. Thus, the Israelites were introduced to Baal worship, which the successful farmers of Canaan testified was the secret of fertile soil, sunshine and rain, and good crops. The Canaanites also introduced the Israelites to the sexual orgies associated with Baal worship. Not surprisingly, many Israelites were attracted to a religion that promised material success and promoted sexual pleasure. They were willing to forsake their ancient God of the desert with His strict moral code for a god that promised prosperity and pleasure.

2. Punishment (2:14–15)

> **14 And the anger of the LORD was hot against Israel, and he delivered them into the hands of spoilers that spoiled them, and he sold them into the hands of their enemies round about, so that they could not any longer stand before their enemies.**
>
> **15 Whithersoever they went out, the hand of the LORD was against them for evil, as the LORD had said, and as the LORD had sworn unto them: and they were greatly distressed.**

God's anger burned against such flagrant sins and such callous forsaking of the Lord. God could have punished them directly, but He chose to let them reap what they had sown. When Israel faithfully served the Lord, His presence guided and protected them. Often He had given them victory over enemies much stronger than they. When Israel forsook the Lord, the Lord withdrew His protection. He left them in the hands of the gods in which they trusted. The problem for Israel was that these nonexistent gods were powerless to help Israel. Israel's enemies began to attack and defeat the Israelites. At times, the Lord even aided the enemies. As the book of Judges bears out, many of these enemies were from nations "round about" Canaan.

None of these disasters would have surprised the Israelites if they had remembered the Law of God and the warnings of leaders like Moses and Joshua. Before Israel had entered Canaan, Moses had set before them life and death (Deut. 30:15–20). If they obeyed the Lord, He promised life; if they forsook Him, He warned of death and ruin. This is the meaning of the words "as the LORD had sworn unto them."

When God punishes His people, He does so to call them back to Him. Although this is not spelled out in verses 14–15, it is implied in the severe distress that the Lord sent on them.

3. Deliverance (2:16–18)

> **16 Nevertheless the LORD raised up judges, which delivered them out of the hand of those that spoiled them.**
>
> **17 And yet they would not hearken unto their judges, but they went a whoring after other gods, and bowed themselves unto them: they turned quickly out of the way which their fathers walked in, obeying the commandments of the LORD, but they did not so.**
>
> **18 And when the LORD raised them up judges, then the LORD was with the judge, and delivered them out of the hand of their enemies all the days of the judge: for it repented the LORD because of their groanings by reason of them that oppressed them and vexed them.**

The Lord showed compassion on the people in their afflictions and sent deliverance. The word *repented* in verse 18 means that God was moved with pity on them and acted to help them. Nothing explicit is said

in verse 18 about the people repenting of their sins, but two factors lead us to assume that their repentance was involved:
1. The final words of verse 18 suggest this. Their groanings, which moved the Lord to pity, likely included prayers for divine help.
2. The book of Judges gives examples of a cycle that includes the people's cries for help (see Judg. 3:9, 15; 4:3; 6:6; 10:10).

The divine deliverance came in the form of human leaders called judges. We think of a judge in terms of courts and trials, and some of the judges did make judicial decisions. However, the judges were primarily deliverers. Some were civil and political leaders, but some were ordinary people whom the Lord called and empowered for a specific task. Most of the judges led military actions against Israel's enemies. At least one judge, Deborah, was a woman prophetess and judge. Samson was also a judge, as was Gideon. Samuel was also considered a judge; but he is so associated with the beginning of the kingdom that his story is in the book of 1 Samuel, not in Judges.

The judges were empowered by the Spirit of God (Judg. 3:10; 6:34; 11:29; 14:6, 19; 15:14). The Spirit came upon judges in times of crisis to equip them for specific tasks. The work of the Spirit in the lives of the judges was thus somewhat different from the abiding presence of the Spirit in the lives of Christians.

Verse 17 shows that the obedience of the people was imperfect even during the lifetime of the judges. The people's sin is described as spiritual adultery because the Israelites followed after other gods like an unfaithful spouse turns from a husband or wife. The Old Testament describes the Lord as Israel's husband and Israel as an unfaithful wife (see Hos. 2–3). This description of their sin was especially appropriate for Baal worship in which sexual immorality expressed spiritual adultery.

4. Downward spiral of sin (2:19)

19 And it came to pass, when the judge was dead, that they returned, and corrupted themselves more than their fathers, in following other gods to serve them, and to bow down unto them; they ceased not from their own doings, nor from their stubborn way.

This verse explains why the deadly process became a cycle that was repeated over and over. Even during the lifetime of a judge, the people's devotion was mixed with idolatry; however, after a judge died, the people reverted to their former practices. In fact, they did things that were worse than their fathers had done. So the cycle was a spiral downward to a lower level of moral and spiritual depravity. Chapters 3–16 show how this deadly cycle was repeated in spite of many punishments, prayers for help, and divine deliverances.

As the period of the judges unfolded, the people's repentance seems to have become increasingly superficial as their moral and spiritual condition deteriorated. The word translated "stubborn" can also be translated "stiff-necked." The people became increasingly hardened and obstinate in their evil ways.

5. Renewed punishment (2:20–23)
20 And the anger of the LORD was hot against Israel.

Notice that the opening words of verse 20 are the same as the opening words of verse 14. The people's return to sin led the Lord to pour out His wrath on them again. As someone has said, "Those who refuse to learn the lessons of history are doomed to repeat the mistakes of the past." The people should have learned from the past that the wages of sin is death; but as soon as the immediate danger was past, they returned to their sinful ways. In most cases, the sinners in verse 19 were a new generation; but in some cases they were the ones who had sinned, been punished, repented, and been delivered—yet they started the cycle over again. This shows (1) the powerful hold of sin on human beings and (2) the certainty of punishment for sin.

The Israelites had failed to completely drive out the pagan people of Canaan. The influence of these pagans and their gods were a constant snare to the Israelites (2:3). The Lord allowed them to remain as a test of the people's faith and loyalty to Him—a test they failed repeatedly during the period of the judges (2:21–23).

SUMMARY OF BIBLE TRUTHS

1. The basic sin of turning from God leads to a variety of sins.
2. Persistent sin and impenitence brings judgment.
3. When God's people cry out, He hears and helps them.
4. After a crisis is over, many people return to their sins.
5. With each cycle of sin, the sin becomes worse.

APPLYING THE BIBLE

1. The cycle of sin and repentance. The commentary on today's lesson lists four stages of the continuing cycle in Israel's response to God: Sin, punishment, repentance, deliverance.
- Where would you place America today in that cycle?
- Is it possible that the various stages overlap somewhat?
- Where would you place your church today in that cycle?
- Where would you place *yourself* in that cycle?

2. The day of prayer. A recent American president called for a national day of fasting and prayer in order to seek God's blessings on us as a nation. A religious official was quoted widely in the media as saying that the president had no right whatever to issue such a plea. Think about these questions:
- Is it right and proper to set aside such special days? (It might be asked: What are the chief indications that we need such days?)
- Who should call for such observations?
- What is the benefit of such days?
- What if certain individuals did not need to repent and turn to God? Should they participate?
- Should we wait to seek God's blessings on our country until such special days are called?

October 4, 1998

3. The self-destruction of Rome. British historian Edward Gibbon is remembered for his classic *The Decline and Fall of the Roman Empire*. Gibbon described Rome's intricate government, majestic cities, and knowledgeable citizens, but he concluded that the Romans essentially destroyed themselves. If Gibbon is right, money and power and knowledge are not enough to save nations.

4. Learning from the Bible. President William McKinley once voiced what many students of history believe: "The more profoundly we study this wonderful Book (the Bible), and the more closely we observe its divine precepts, the better citizens we will become and the higher will be our destiny as a nation."[1] That is the essential lesson of all biblical history, particularly that portion we focus on in our study of this lesson.

5. The danger of riches.

- "In this world there are only two tragedies. One is not getting what one wants, and the other is getting it" (Oscar Wilde).
- "War destroys men, but luxury destroys mankind; at once corrupts the body and the mind" (John Crowne).
- "On the soft bed of luxury most kingdoms have expired" (Edward Young).
- "Luxury is the first, second and third cause of the fall of republics. It is the vampire which soothes us into a fatal slumber while it sucks the lifeblood of our veins" (Edward Payson).

6. National decline. The lapse of morals is always at the heart of national decline.

- "History fails to record a single precedent in which nations subject to moral decay have not passed into political and economic decline" (General Douglas MacArthur).
- "Only a virtuous people are capable of freedom. As nations become corrupt and vicious, they have more need of masters" (Benjamin Franklin).

7. The downward road. National decline is never sudden, even if it appears to be that way. (On several occasions in Revelation 18, it is noted that Babylon's judgment is swift and sudden—see vv. 10, 19—but she had been spiraling downward for a long time, perhaps imperceptibly to her inhabitants.) "The safest road to Hell is the gradual one—the gentle slope, soft underfoot, without sudden turnings, without milestones, without signposts."[2] Where is our nation on such a slippery slope? Where is your church on such a slippery slope? And yourself?

8. Revival is always necessary. Theodore Roosevelt once remarked, "We must have—I believe we have already—a genuine and permanent moral awakening, without which no wisdom of legislation or administration really means anything."[3] Is it possible for a nation to experience a "permanent moral awakening"? If not, what does that imply about a continuing call for revival? What is the church's place in all that? (I once heard a revival preacher say, "Revivals are like baths; you can't do it once and for all!")

TEACHING THE BIBLE

October 4 1998

- *Main Idea*: Israel's cycle between sin and judgment demonstrates how God handles our sin.
- *Suggested Teaching Aim:* To lead adults to repent and confess their sin.

A TEACHING OUTLINE

Cycle of Sin and Judgment

I. From Obedience to Disobedience (Judg. 2:1–2)
   1. Punishment for disobedience (2:1–5)
   2. Flashback to better days (2:6–10)
II. A Deadly Cycle (Judg. 2:11–23)
   1. Sin (2:11–13)
   2. Punishment (2:14–15)
   3. Deliverance (2:16–18)
   4. Downward spiral of sin (2:19)
   5. Renewed punishment (2:20–23)

Introduce the Bible Study

Use "The downward road" from "Applying the Bible" to introduce the lesson. Ask members to be thinking about the answers to these questions as you move through the lesson.

Search for Biblical Truth

Briefly summarize the material in "Studying the Bible" on Judges 2:1–10 to set the context. **IN ADVANCE**, copy the six "Summary of Bible Truths" on large strips of paper. Organize your class into five groups and give paper and pencils to each group. Place the first strip on the wall and ask members to read it silently. Ask someone to read Judges 2:11–13. Define *Baalim, Baal,* and *Ashtaroth* and point out how Israel worshiped these gods instead of the Lord. Relate the two expectations God had for Israel when He established the covenant with them. Ask the first group to be thinking of a case study they can write based on the Bible truth on the strip.

Place the second truth on the wall and ask a member to read Judges 2:14–15. Summarize the material in "Studying the Bible" to explain these verses. Ask the second group to be thinking of a case study they can write based on the Bible truth on the second strip.

Place the third truth on the wall and ask a member to read Judges 2:16–18. Point out (1) the two factors that indicate Israel repented; (2) the role of the judge; (3) why Israel's sin was described as spiritual adultery. Ask the third group to be thinking of a case study they can write based on the Bible truth on the third strip.

Place the fourth truth on the wall and ask a member to read Judges 2:19. Explain (1) the downward spiral Israel was in; (2) their spiritual deterioration described in the word *stubborn*. Ask the fourth group to be

October 4, 1998

thinking of a case study they can write based on the Bible truth on the fourth strip.

Place the fifth truth on the wall and ask a member to read Judges 2:20. Read this quote: "Those who refuse to learn the lessons of history are doomed to repeat the mistakes of the past." Explain God's repeated punishment. Ask the fifth group to be thinking of a case study they can write based on the Bible truth on the fourth strip.

Give the Truth a Personal Focus

Allow groups time to write a contemporary case study that illustrates their Bible truth. Call on each group to read their case study aloud without additional comment.

Ask, Based upon your life this past week, if you had lived in ancient Israel, would you have helped or hindered Israel's cycle of sin and judgment?

Ask members to spend a time of silence as they confess their sin to God and repent of it. Close with a prayer that our nation will not have to repeat the process Israel went through.

---

1. Quote from Stephen Northrop, *A Cloud of Witnesses* (Portland, Oreg.: American Heritage Ministries, 1987), 313.
2. From C. S. Lewis, *The Screwtape Letters,* cited from *Bartlett's Familiar Quotations,* Thirteenth Edition, 980.
3. Theodore Roosevelt, quoted in Richard Heffner, ed., *A Documentary History of the United States* (New York: New American Library of World Literature, 1961), 225.

From Judges to Kings

October 11 1998

Background Passage: 1 Samuel 7:15–8:22
Focal Passages: 1 Samuel 7:15–8:9,19–22

This lesson provides a bridge between two periods of Old Testament history: The period of the judges and the period of the united kingdom. Samuel was the last of the judges, but his story is in 1 Samuel because he was also reluctantly involved in the beginning of Israel as a kingdom. This lesson focuses on that traumatic transition.

▶**Study Aim:** *To contrast the attitudes of Samuel and the elders of Israel toward having a king.*

STUDYING THE BIBLE

OUTLINE AND SUMMARY
 I. The Last Judges (1 Sam. 7:15–8:3)
   1. Samuel—model of a good judge (7:15–17)
   2. Samuel's sons—bad judges (8:1–3)
 II. Request for a King (1 Sam. 8:4–22)
   1. The elders' request (8:4–5)
   2. Samuel's prayer (8:6–9)
   3. Samuel's warning (8:10–18)
   4. Israel's insistence (8:19–20)
   5. The Lord's decision (8:21–22)

Samuel was a model judge throughout his life (7:15–17). His greedy sons took bribes and perverted justice (8:1–3). Elders from all the tribes told Samuel they wanted a king (8:4–5). The Lord told Samuel to grant their request, but to warn them of the disadvantages (8:6–9). Samuel warned the people of conscription and taxes under a king (8:10–18). Still the people felt that a king could judge the whole nation and lead them into battle (8:19–20). The Lord told Samuel to grant their request for a king (8:21–22).

I. The Last Judges (1 Sam. 7:15–8:3)
1. Samuel—model of a good judge (7:15–17)

15 And Samuel judged Israel all the days of his life.

16 And he went from year to year in circuit to Bethel, and Gilgal, and Mizpeh, and judged Israel in all those places.

17 And his return was to Ramah; for there was his house; and there he judged Israel; and there he built an altar unto the LORD.

First Samuel 1–7 tells the story of one of the key personalities in the Bible. Samuel was born in answer to the prayers of a barren woman and dedicated by her to the Lord (1 Sam. 1). As a child, he served at the tabernacle at Shiloh [SHIGH loh], where Eli was priest and judge (1 Sam. 2). God called young Samuel as a prophet to deliver a painful message to Eli (1 Sam. 3). After the death of Eli's wicked sons and Eli himself,

October 11, 1998

Samuel became leader. He summoned the Israelites and led them to defeat the Philistines [fih LISS teens] (1 Sam. 7:2–14).

Thus, Samuel served as a judge throughout all the days of his life. His duties included those of a circuit judge who lived and judged at Ramah [RAY muh] but who also went to Bethel, Gilgal, and Mizpeh [MIZ puh]. Ramah was the birthplace of Samuel (1:19). Bethel was where Jacob had made his vow to the Lord (Gen. 28:19). Gilgal was the location of the memorial of the crossing of the Jordan (Josh. 4:20). Mizpeh was the site of a stone erected by Samuel to commemorate the Lord's victory over the Philistines (1 Sam. 7:12).

Samuel was noted for his devotion to the Lord. His sensitivity to the Lord is seen in his response to the Lord's call when he was only a child (1 Sam. 3:1–10). Samuel's devotion was expressed in his prayers and in his commitment to worship. He built an altar at his home in Ramah in order to worship the Lord.

2. Samuel's sons—bad judges (8:1–3)

1 And it came to pass, when Samuel was old, that he made his sons judges over Israel.

2 Now the name of his firstborn was Joel; and the name of the second, Abiah: they were judges in Beersheba.

3 And his sons walked not in his ways, but turned aside after lucre, and took bribes, and perverted judgment.

Samuel was an old man who must have thought that his days were about ended. He even turned over the duties of judge to his sons. Samuel's two sons—Joel and Abiah [uh BIGH uh]—were as evil as Samuel was good. The word translated "lucre" means "gain from violence or dishonesty." The word translated "judgment" means "justice." They sought money for themselves at any price; thus, they took bribes to pervert justice in favor of those who paid the bribes. The Lord commanded judges to be totally impartial in their verdicts, just as the Lord Himself is (Deut. 1:16–17). He condemned judges who favored the rich and powerful at the expense of the poor and powerless (Deut. 16:19). These sins were later strongly condemned by prophets (Amos 5:12).

The Bible does not tell us why Samuel named his sons as judges, nor does it tell how Samuel responded to their sins. Samuel should have learned from Eli's tragic experience with evil sons in places of authority (see 1 Sam. 2:12–36; 3:12–18; 4). Being a judge was not ordinarily a hereditary office. When the people tried to make Gideon a king with a dynasty, Gideon refused, saying, "I will not rule over you, neither shall my son rule over you: the LORD shall rule over you" (Judg. 8:23). Samuel surely agreed with Gideon that a judge was not to become a king because he believed as Gideon did that Israel was to be a theocracy, a nation where God ruled. However, Samuel apparently saw no problem in naming his sons as judges.

Although Samuel's sons were at Beersheba [BEE ehr SHE buh], Samuel surely knew of their evil actions. When the elders of Israel reported this to him, Samuel did not dispute their report (8:5). Surely Samuel was displeased by their actions, and he very likely tried to restrain them. However, their evil became one reason for the elders' request for a king.

II. Request for a King (1 Sam. 8:4–22)

1. The elders' request (8:4–5)

> 4 Then all the elders of Israel gathered themselves together, and came to Samuel unto Ramah,
>
> 5 And said unto him, Behold, thou art old, and thy sons walk not in thy ways: now make us a king to judge us like all the nations.

The elders in each community were the respected leaders who met at the city gate to arbitrate disputes and oversee the affairs of the community. Verse 4 speaks of "all the elders of Israel," which would be a large group of influential leaders. The fact that they came from all the tribes showed that their request represented the feeling of all the tribes.

The life of Israel during the period of the judges was intended to be a theocracy, a people over whom God ruled. The judges were not kings, whose descendants succeeded them. Most of the judges were deliverers for only some of the tribes (Judg. 5:15–17; 8:1; 12:1). Samuel may be the only exception, for he issued a call for "all Israel" to fight the Philistines (7:5). And the fact that elders came to him from "all Israel" supports that view.

The elders agreed that they wanted a king to be their ruler. They pointed out that Samuel was old, in order to show Samuel that their request was not because of any failing on his part. The naming of his sons as judges and their wicked behavior was cited as one reason for wanting a king. However, their main reason was that they wanted to be like other nations.

They later elaborated on their reasons (8:20), but basically they felt the need for a central authority to replace the loose confederation of the tribes of the time of the judges. They had no argument with a theocracy in theory, but they believed it had not worked out well in practice.

2. Samuel's prayer (8:6–9)

> 6 But the thing displeased Samuel, when they said, Give us a king to judge us. And Samuel prayed unto the LORD.
>
> 7 And the LORD said unto Samuel, Hearken unto the voice of the people in all that they say unto thee: for they have not rejected thee, but they have rejected me, that I should not reign over them.
>
> 8 According to all the works which they have done since the day that I brought them up out of Egypt even unto this day, wherewith they have forsaken me, and served other gods, so do they also unto thee.
>
> 9 Now therefore hearken unto their voice: howbeit yet protest solemnly unto them, and shew them the manner of the king that shall reign over them.

October 11 1998

Not surprisingly, Samuel was displeased by their request. However, before responding, he took the matter to the Lord in prayer. As we have seen, Samuel was a man of prayer.

The Lord told Samuel three things:

1. The Lord assured Samuel that this request was directed against Him, and not against Samuel. The Lord cited this as typical of their rebellion since coming out of Egypt. The Lord clearly saw this as a rejection of the ideal of theocracy, in which the Lord rules over His people.
2. The Lord told Samuel to hearken to their request. That is, he was to grant their request and let them have their way.
3. The Lord told Samuel to tell them of the disadvantages of having a king.

3. Samuel's warning (8:10–18)

They wanted more central authority, but they would pay a heavy price for having a king. Their sons would be conscripted by the king for military duty or for labor (8:10–12). Their daughters would also be conscripted for work (8:13). The best of their crops would be taken, and all their crops would be taxed (8:14–15). Their servants and their livestock would be taken at the king's pleasure as well as taxed (8:16–17). When these things happened, the people would cry out to the Lord; but He would not hear them (8:18).

4. Israel's insistence (8:19–20)

> 19 Nevertheless the people refused to obey the voice of Samuel; and they said, Nay; but we will have a king over us;
>
> 20 That we also may be like all the nations; and that our king may judge us, and go out before us, and fight our battles.

The people patiently listened to Samuel, but they still insisted on having a king. They cited three reasons, which in their opinion outweighed the arguments against having a king:

1. They wanted to be like other nations.
2. They wanted the king to judge over them.
3. They wanted a king to fight their battles for them.

The second reason meant that they wanted some central authority to weld the loosely knit, often competitive tribes into one nation. Judges 17–21 tells of the anarchy that sometimes marked the period of the judges. The writer explained it by saying, "In those days there was no king in Israel: every man did that which was right in his own eyes" (Judg. 21:25; see also 17:6; 18:1; 19:1).

Their third reason related to warfare. Ancient kings like Saul and David led their armies into battle; and often (especially in David's case) won victories. However, kings did not fight alone. As Samuel had told them, kings conscripted young men to be soldiers. Only a few generations after their request for a king, the people also chafed under the heavy weight of conscripted labor and heavy taxes under Solomon (1 Kings 12:4).

October 11 1998

5. The Lord's decision (8:21–22)

> 21 And Samuel heard all the words of the people, and he rehearsed them in the ears of the LORD.
>
> 22 And the LORD said to Samuel, Hearken unto their voice, and make them a king. And Samuel said unto the men of Israel, Go ye every man unto his city.

The Lord gave Samuel two commands: (1) let them have their king; and (2) accept responsibility for helping make a king. Samuel probably thought his life was about over; however, his usefulness to the Lord was soon to enter a new stage. Samuel spent the rest of his life fulfilling that second command, as 1 Samuel 9–24 shows. His role became more that of a prophet. Throughout the period of the kings, prophets played an increasingly important role in calling to account both the kings and the people.

The first command raises deep issues about how the sovereign God works out His will while allowing humans freedom of choice. God did not prefer for Israel to have a king, but He allowed it after clearly warning them of its dangers. God continued to operate as the Lord within this new political structure in Israel.

SUMMARY OF BIBLE TRUTHS

1. Some people serve the Lord from childhood to old age.
2. Sometimes, people of true faith have rebellious, ungodly children.
3. God warns of the consequences of unwise choices.
4. The sovereign God allows people freedom to make their own decisions, but God allows them to reap what they sow.

APPLYING THE BIBLE

1. Who's in charge here? Today's lesson is about how God wishes to rule His people. I love the story about the two men fighting, for all they were worth, outside a business establishment. A stranger stopped them long enough to ask the name of the owner of the store. Through swollen lips and loose teeth, one of the combatants replied, "You'll have to wait a while; we're trying to decide that right now!" That's not the best way to do it! But our relationship to God boils down to this question: Will we or will we not admit that God is in charge and submit to His rule in our lives?

2. Rejecting God's rule. The people of Samuel's day believed that God's government through the judges had failed. Actually, His government had not failed; it had been found difficult and discarded. When God's government doesn't work, it always comes down to this: "They have not rejected thee, but they have rejected me, that I should not reign over them" (1 Sam. 8:7).

3. Human nature is the real problem. William Temple once said, "There is no structured organization of society which can bring about the coming of the Kingdom of God on earth, since all systems can be perverted by the selfishness of man." In fact, if history teaches us anything, it is that people will pervert any system of government. Any system of

October 11 1998

government would work if both the ruler and the ruled would obey God! That includes a monarchy (the rule of a king or queen), an oligarchy (the rule of a few), an aristocracy (the rule of an elite group), a democracy (the rule of the people), a representative democracy (the rule of representatives of the people, as in America), a matriarchy (the rule of women), or a patriarchy (the rule of men), even a plutocracy (the rule of the rich)! The problem with all governments is human nature!

4. No perfect society. In 1955 William Golding wrote a very interesting novel entitled *The Lord of the Flies*. It is a story about a group of boys marooned on a beautiful and pristine island. They set up what they believed to be the perfect government, "from scratch." Guess what? The story ends, after immense political intrigue by the various power groups that developed among the boys, with their pristine island brought to ruins and incapable of sustaining human life. Sound familiar?

5. Obedience to God. "There is one proposition in which the whole matter, as it is relevant to human duty, may be summed up; that all our works, alike inward and outward, great and small, ought to be done in obedience to God." The eminent English statesman William Gladstone said that. Samuel knew that long ago. Obedience to God is the supreme virtue in government, whether of the self or the state.

6. What is the best thing about heaven? Perhaps the best thing about heaven is that "the throne of God and of the Lamb shall be in it; and his servants shall serve him" (Rev. 22:3). Perfect administration (God and the Lamb on the throne) and perfect subordination (all His servants obeying Him) equals perfect regulation!

7. Encouraging our children to obey God. Freckles are biologically transmissible, but faith is not! If everybody on earth were Christians, we would still be but a single generation from everybody on earth being pagans, because, again, the faith is not biologically transmissible! The call for a king and all the sadness of Israel's succeding story begins with Samuel's sinful sons (see 1 Sam. 8:5). Contrast Samuel's family with that of Timothy. Paul began a letter to Timothy by mentioning "the unfeigned faith that is in thee, which dwelt first in thy grandmother Lois, and thy mother Eunice" (2 Tim. 1:5). List five things we can do to encourage our children and youth to walk in obedience to God.

8. Lifetime of stewardship. What a great gift to Israel Samuel was! He walked with God all his life. How long do you intend to walk with God? I once heard a retiree give a stewardship testimony. In the course of his brief and simple testimony, he said, without any fanfare, that it had been his privilege to tithe his income to the Lord for seventy-five years! I went home that night, got on my knees in the bedroom, and asked God for the privilege of being able to say that same sentence someday.

9. Think about it.

- Where is it, in your view, that our government is in rebellion against God?

- Where is it, in your own life, that you are in rebellion against God's government?

TEACHING THE BIBLE

October 11 1998

▸ *Main Idea:* Israel's move from being led by judges to having kings shows how God can work even in less-than-desirable situations.
▸ *Suggested Teaching Aim:* To lead adults to identify how God works in their lives even when they have not lived up to His plan for them.

A TEACHING OUTLINE

From Judges to Kings

I. *The Last Judges (1 Sam. 7:15–8:3)*
   1. *Samuel—model of a good judge (7:15–17)*
   2. *Samuel's sons—bad judges (8:1–3)*
II. *Request for a King (1 Sam. 8:4–22)*
   1. *The elders' request (8:4–5)*
   2. *Samuel's prayer (8:6–9)*
   3. *Samuel's warning (8:10–18)*
   4. *Israel's insistence (8:19–20)*
   5. *The Lord's decision (8:21–22)*

Introduce the Bible Study

Use "Who's in charge here" in "Applying The Bible" to introduce the lesson. Point out that today's lesson describes how Israel moved from being led by judges to having a king. This move caused an ongoing debate over how Israel would be ruled.

Search for Biblical Truth

IN ADVANCE, make a poster using the above "Teaching Outline." Cover the points with strips of paper until you are ready to teach them. Summarize the seven summary statements in "Outline and Summary" to set the context.

IN ADVANCE, enlist two members to summarize the material in the two outline subpoints under "I. The Last Judges." Uncover "1. Samuel—model of a good judge (7:15–17)." Ask someone to read 1 Samuel 7:15–17. Call for the member to summarize this point. Uncover "2. Samuel's sons—bad judges (8:1–3)." Ask someone to read 1 Samuel 8:1–3. Call for the second member to summarize this point.

Uncover "II. 1. The elder's request." Ask someone to read 8:4–5. Using the material in "Studying the Bible," lecture briefly covering the following: (1) the role of judge in Israel and (2) the three reasons the elders gave for wanting a king.

Uncover "2. Samuel's prayer." Ask someone to read 8:6–9. Lecture briefly covering the following: (1) Samuel's displeasure with Israel; (2) the three things the Lord told Samuel.

Uncover subpoints 3 and 4 on the outline. Briefly relate the material in "Studying the Bible" on 8:10–18. Call for someone to read 8:19–20. Using the material in "Studying the Bible," lecture briefly on the three reasons Israel wanted a king.

October 11, 1998

Uncover subpoint 5 on the outline. Call for someone to read 8:21–22. Using the material in "Studying the Bible" on 8:21–22, lecture briefly on the two commands the Lord gave Samuel.

IN ADVANCE, copy the four statements in "Summary of Bible Truths" and distribute to four members. Ask them to read the statements.

Give the Truth a Personal Focus

Say: God gave Israel what they wanted, even though it was not His perfect will. Yet God used the kingship to accomplish His will. What was the greatest event that came as a direct result of the kingship? (Christ the King.)

Say: As God used Israel's desires to bring good, so He can use for good decisions we make that may not be best. Can anyone share with us an experience in your life in which God has done this? (Try to think of a situation in your own life to share to get the discussion going.)

Point out that God is not limited by our mistakes. He can accomplish His will regardless of what we do. We may suffer (as Israel did under their kings), but God can and does override our decisions to accomplish His will.

Have a time of prayer. **IN ADVANCE**, enlist two members to lead this prayer. Ask one to pray that all would be sensitive to following God's will. Ask the second to pray that even when members fail to follow God's will that God will use them to accomplish His will.

Jeroboam's Sin

October
18
1998

Background Passage: 1 Kings 12
Focal Passages: 1 Kings 12:20, 25–33

This lesson, like last Sunday's lesson, bridges two periods of Old Testament history. First Kings 12 marks the end of the united kingdom and the beginning of the divided kingdom. Rehoboam [ree hoh BOH uhm] and Jeroboam [jer uh BOH uhm] are the key personalities in the break between the northern and southern tribes. We are focusing on Jeroboam and his sin, which eventually ruined Israel.

▶**Study Aim:** *To explain what Jeroboam did and why it was sinful.*

STUDYING THE BIBLE

OUTLINE AND SUMMARY
I. **Rehoboam Loses the United Kingdom (1 Kings 12:1–24)**
   1. The northern tribes make a request (12:1–5)
   2. Rehoboam refuses their request (12:6–15)
   3. The northern tribes rebel (12:16–20)
   4. Rehoboam heeds a warning against civil war (12:21–24)
II. **Jeroboam Sets a Pattern of Sin (1 Kings 12:25–33)**
   1. Builds two cities (12:25)
   2. Fears Israel will return to Judah (12:26–27)
   3. Sets up two golden calves (12:28–30)
   4. Devises his own religious practices (12:31–33)

The northern tribes asked Rehoboam to ease the heavy burdens laid on them by Solomon (12:1–5). Rehoboam rejected their request (12:6–15). The northern tribes rebelled and named Jeroboam as their king (12:16–20). Rehoboam heeded a warning against attacking the northern tribes (12:21–24). Jeroboam built a capital at Shechem (12:25). He feared that the hearts of the people would return to Rehoboam if they went to Jerusalem to worship (12:26–27). Therefore, he set up golden calves at Bethel and Dan (12:28–30). He named priests who were not from the tribe of Levi, and he changed the date for the Feast of Tabernacles (12:31–33).

I. Rehoboam Loses the United Kingdom (1 Kings 12:1–14)

1. The northern tribes make a request (12:1–5)

The three successive kings of the united kingdom were Saul, David, and Solomon. Israel reached its greatest worldly power and fame under Solomon. However, this golden age had its downside for the common people who paid the high taxes and furnished the labor for Solomon's vast enterprises. The northern tribes, who had never been enthusiastic about serving the house of David, especially chafed under this heavy burden. Thus, after Solomon died, Rehoboam went to the northern city of Shechem expecting to be named as king. Instead, Rehoboam was confronted with a firm request that he reduce the heavy burden the people had been forced to bear under Solomon. Rehoboam asked for three days before responding to their request.

2. Rehoboam refuses their request (12:6–15)

Rehoboam had two sets of counselors: The older counselors, who had advised Solomon, and the younger counselors, with whom he had grown up. The older men told the king that if he showed himself sensitive to the people's grievances that the people would loyally follow him. The younger group advised Rehoboam to demonstrate his strength by threatening to make their burdens even greater. Rehoboam heeded the advice of the younger group. Therefore, at the end of three days, the king told the disgruntled northern tribes that he was going to add to their burden and increase their punishments.

3. The northern tribes rebel (12:16–20)

> 20 And it came to pass, when all Israel heard that Jeroboam was come again, that they sent and called him unto the congregation, and made him king over all Israel: there was none that followed the house of David, but the tribe of Judah only.

Not surprisingly, the northern tribes exploded into rebellion against Rehoboam. Then the king made another foolish mistake. He sent the man who had been the chief administrator of the heavy burdens to talk to the northern tribes. They stoned him to death. Then the northern tribes summoned Jeroboam and made him their king.

Let's go back and summarize what we know about Jeroboam up to this point. He was an industrious young man whom Solomon appointed as overseer (11:28). The prophet Ahijah (uh HIGH juh] predicted to Jeroboam that God would make him king over ten of the tribes of Israel. The Lord also promised to make Jeroboam's house a permanent dynasty in Israel if Jeroboam obeyed the Lord (11:29–39). Later Jeroboam led a rebellion against Solomon and was forced to flee to Egypt when the revolt failed (11:26, 40). Jeroboam returned from Egypt after the death of Solomon and was present when the northern tribes made their request of Rehoboam (12:2–3). He led the delegation that heard the king reject the request (12:12). Therefore, the people turned to Jeroboam to be their king.

Verse 20 says that only Judah followed Rehoboam; however, other references show that all or most of Benjamin also was loyal to David's house (11:35; 12:21, 23).

From this point on, there were two kingdoms instead of one. The immediate cause of the division was the foolish refusal by Rehoboam of the people's request, but Solomon had created the problem that led to the request. In addition, the northern tribes were never fully content under the reign of David and Solomon. During much of Saul's reign, David and the people of his home tribe of Judah were in rebellion against Saul. After Saul's death, the northern tribes supported Saul's son as their king until circumstances of war forced them to yield to David's rule. Even when they did, it was only after the elders of Israel had reached some kind of understanding with David (2 Samuel 2:8–11; 3:1; 5:1–3).

4. Rehoboam heeds a warning against civil war (12:21–24)

Rehoboam gathered his troops to attack the northern tribes; however, a prophet warned him and the people of Judah not to fight against their brothers in Israel. Rehoboam and the people of Judah obeyed the Lord and returned to their homes.

II. Jeroboam Sets a Pattern of Sin (1 Kings 12:25–33)
1. Builds two cities (12:25)

> 25 Then Jeroboam built Shechem in mount Ephraim, and dwelt therein; and went out from thence, and built Penuel.

Shechem [SHEK uhm] was located in north central Israel in the territory of the tribe of Ephraim [EE frih uhm], the largest of the ten northern tribes. This was where Abram first stopped when he entered Canaan (Gen. 12:6). When Jacob returned to Canaan, he settled at Shechem (Gen. 33:18–19). Joshua led Israel to renew their vows to the Lord at Shechem (Josh. 24:1–17). This was where the northern tribes had made their request of Rehoboam (1 Kings 12:1). Therefore, Jeroboam chose an ancient site on which to build his capital city.

Penuel [PEN yoo uhl] was another city that Jeroboam built. It was on the other side of the Jordan River.

2. Fears Israel will return to Judah (12:26–27)

> 26 And Jeroboam said in his heart, Now shall the kingdom return to the house of David:
>
> 27 If this people go up to do sacrifice in the house of the LORD at Jerusalem, then shall the heart of this people turn again unto their lord, even unto Rehoboam king of Judah, and they shall kill me, and go again to Rehoboam king of Judah.

Since all the people were supposed to worship at the central sanctuary and since the sanctuary was the new temple built by Solomon at Jerusalem, Jeroboam feared what would happen if the Israelites continued to go to Jerusalem to worship. They would begin to think of Rehoboam as their king, and they would then kill Jeroboam. Notice how insecure Jeroboam felt as soon as he got power. His later actions were motivated by self-interest and political expediency.

Notice also that the Southern Kingdom was now called Judah. Verse 21 shows that the name *Israel* was retained by the northern tribes. The Northern Kingdom came to be called the kingdom of Israel.

3. Sets up two golden calves (12:28–30)

> 28 Whereupon the king took counsel, and made two calves of gold, and said unto them, It is too much for you to go up to Jerusalem: behold thy gods, O Israel, which brought thee up out of the land of Egypt.
>
> 29 And he set one in Bethel, and the other put he in Dan.

October 18, 1998

30 And this thing became a sin: for the people went to worship before the one, even unto Dan.

Jeroboam sought advice and decided to build two places of worship in the Northern Kingdom: One at Bethel near the southern border and the other in the north at Dan. These two sites had the advantage of a history as places of worship. Bethel had been a worship place for Abram (Gen. 12:8) and Jacob (Gen. 28:10–22; 35:1–3). The ark had been kept there for a time (Judg. 20:27). There was already an image at Dan (Judg. 18:30–31). Verse 30 is usually translated in such a way as to include worship at Bethel as well as Dan.

Jeroboam decided to erect a golden calf at each of these sites. He was probably influenced by the fact that many of the religions of the area considered the bull as an image of their god. The Syrians even used the bull to represent the supreme god El. Jeroboam tried to identify these worship sites as places to worship the gods or God who brought them out of Egypt. {Keep in mind that the word translated "God" is plural and is often translated "gods."} Thus, it seems that Jeroboam wanted a religion that worshipers of the Lord could use and also one that could be used by people who wanted to combine the worship of several gods.

The Bible brands this moral and spiritual compromise as sin. Even if we assume that Jeroboam intended these as places to worship the Lord, they violated the second commandment. God cannot be worshiped by images. The incident with the golden calf at Mount Sinai should have served as a warning to Jeroboam (Exod. 32). Jeroboam used the same fateful words that Aaron had used to summon people to worship through the golden calf (Exod. 32:4). Aaron had tried to justify that as "a feast to the LORD" (Exod. 32:5).

Later history shows that the worship at Bethel and Dan eventually became clear violations of the first commandment. Since the bull was a familiar symbol of the fertility religions of the region, Baal worshipers turned these shrines to their own purposes. The prophets Amos and Hosea addressed the sins committed at Bethel and Dan. They condemned the hypocrisy of those who tried to worship the Lord in this way, and they condemned the growing pagan idolatry.

4. Devises his own religious practices (12:31–33)

31 And he made an house of high places, and made priests of the lowest of the people, which were not of the sons of Levi.

32 And Jeroboam ordained a feast in the eighth month, on the fifteenth day of the month, like unto the feast that is in Judah, and he offered upon the altar. So did he in Bethel, sacrificing unto the calves that he had made: and he placed in Bethel the priests of the high places which he had made.

33 So he offered upon the altar which he had made in Bethel the fifteenth day of the eighth month, even in the month which he had devised of his own heart; and ordained a feast unto the children of Israel: and he offered upon the altar, and burnt incense.

October 18 1998

Jeroboam not only made his own places of worship in disobedience to the law about the central sanctuary, but he also made his own priests and set his own schedule of feasts in disobedience to the commandments. The Law restricted priestly duties to people from the tribe of Levi, but Jeroboam chose priests differently. The Law set one date for the Feast of Tabernacles, but Jeroboam changed the date.

The key words in verses 31–33 are those that show how Jeroboam devised his own religious practices without regard to the revealed will of God. Notice the words "which he had devised" in verse 33, and the repetition of the words "which he had made."

The Bible charges that Jeroboam set a pattern of sin and idolatry that continued under each successive king of Israel. The theme that runs throughout the history of the Northern Kingdom is that Israel headed for sure ruin "because of the sins of Jeroboam, who did sin, and who made Israel to sin" (14:16).

To sum up Jeroboam's sins:
1. Jeroboam acted out of self-interest and political expedience.
2. Jeroboam set up his own religious practices rather than following the revealed will of God.
3. Jeroboam broke the first two of the Ten Commandments through his moral and spiritual compromise.
4. Jeroboam influenced many generations and set Israel on the road to destruction.

SUMMARY OF BIBLE TRUTHS

1. Foolish people do not recognize good advice.
2. Harsh treatment of others stirs up strife.
3. Sin acts out of self-interest and ignores the revealed will of God.
4. One person's evil influence can influence many others.

APPLYING THE BIBLE

1. Rehoboam's sin. We've all seen the desk motto, "Please don't confuse me with the facts—my mind is already made up." An accounting firm was hiring a new accountant. The company representative asked the first candidate, "What is two plus two?" The young man replied, "Four." The interviewer dismissed him and called for the second candidate. The second candidate also said "Four" and was dismissed. Then the interviewer asked the third candidate, "What is two plus two?" and the third candidate replied, "What would you like them to be?" He was given the job! Rehoboam's sin was like that. His mind was made up. He was plotting to take over the government no matter what advice he heard.

2. Jeroboam's real problem. Jeroboam had a heart problem, not a head problem. Remember that our Lord said, "out of the abundance of the heart the mouth speaketh" (Matt. 12:34). Some friends of mine have a seven-year-old daughter who was a bit mouthy with her mother and was graciously and fairly but firmly disciplined for it. Later the girl explained to her mother what the problem was. She said it was her permanent teeth. When her mother asked what that could mean, the girl

October 18, 1998

Key People and Events—Northern Kingdom of Israel

Evil Influence of Jeroboam I	The kingdom divided with Jeroboam as first king of northern Israel. Jeroboam's calves at Bethel and Dan set an evil example followed by subsequent kings of Israel, who represented several dynasties (1 Kings 11:26–14:20).
Baal Crisis	King Ahab's wife Jezebel tried to replace the worship of the Lord with Baal worship. God used Elijah and later Elisha to pronounce judgment on Ahab and Jezebel (1 Kings 18:28–2 Kings 9:26).
Amos and Hosea	As Israel headed for destruction, final warnings and calls of love came from the prophets Amos and Hosea (2 Kings 14:23–29; Amos; Hosea).
Fall of Israel	Israel was defeated by the Assyrians in 722/21 B.C. The survivors were scattered among the nations by their captors (2 Kings 15:30–17:41).

explained that since her permanent teeth had come in, she could not control her words. The new teeth were to blame. When the mother asked her daughter what she intended to do about those troublesome permanent teeth, the girl, with a bit of exasperation in her voice, said she had no idea what to do with them, but that they sure were causing her a lot of trouble!

That reminds me of a documentary I saw about the island of Bali. In a rite of passage there, young men are made drunk and then, while they are in a stupefied state, the elders file off the sharp points on their teeth to diminish the young men's "animal instincts." Do you think external cures like that are very effective?

3. The power of words. Jeroboam is a living demonstration of the truth stated in Proverbs 15:1: "A soft answer turneth away wrath, but grievous words stir up anger." Can you think of a recent situation which illustrates the dangerous power of speech?

4. The power of evil influence. I once heard about a man who was so mean that he infected a whole county! Think of the influence of Adolph Hitler and Joseph Stalin. Contrast these with Abraham Lincoln and Mother Teresa.

> The smallest breeze that ever blew,
> Some slender grass has wavered;
> And the smallest life I ever knew,
> Some other life has flavored.

How did AIDS happen to America? Researchers have found that, in 1981, physicians in California and New York began to see symptoms that we now identify with AIDS. The researchers found, too, that "a majority of the Los Angeles patients shared a common sexual network. And at the center of this network, they had discovered 'a young man' they called 'Patient Zero' because, as an airline steward, 'he had sown the disease and death all along his route, at the rate of about 250 partners a year.'" What an illustration of the evil influence of one person![1]

5. A word, once spoken, can never be recalled.

> "Never shall thy spoken word
> Be again unsaid, unheard" (Rose Terry Cooke).

"Four things that come not back:
The spoken word;
The sped arrow;
Time past;
The neglected opportunity" (Omar Ibn Al-Harif).

"Eloquence a hundred times has turned the scale of war and peace at will" (Ralph Waldo Emerson).

October 18 1998

6. On the light side.
- I once heard about a country boy who fell into a barrel of molasses. Being a religous lad, he prayed, "Dear Lord, don't let my mouth fail me now!" Rehoboam should have prayed that prayer! And meant it! Not to mention a lot of other folk!
- "A closed mouth gathers no feet."
- "Blessed is the man who, having nothing to say, abstains giving evidence of the fact."

TEACHING THE BIBLE

- *Main Idea:* Selfishness caused the division of the united kingdom.
- *Suggested Teaching Aim:* To lead adults to describe how we use sin to justify our selfish desires.

A TEACHING OUTLINE

Jeroboam's Sin

I. *Rehoboam Loses the United Kingdom (1 Kings 12:1–24)*
  1. *The northern tribes make a request (12:1–5)*
  2. *Rehoboam refuses their request (12:6–15)*
  3. *The northern tribes rebel (12:16–20)*
  4. *Rehoboam heeds a warning against civil war (12:21–24)*

II. *Jeroboam Sets a Pattern of Sin (1 Kings 12:25–33)*
  1. *Builds two cities (12:25)*
  2. *Fears Israel will return to Judah (12:26–27)*
  3. *Sets up two golden calves (12:28–30)*
  4. *Devises his own religious practices (12:31–33)*

Introduce the Bible Study
Use "Rehoboam's sin" in "Applying the Bible" to introduce the Bible study. Read the Main Idea and the Suggested Teaching Aim aloud.

Search for Biblical Truth
IN ADVANCE, make this chart (you will add italicized phrases later):
IN ADVANCE, enlist two people to prepare two- to three-minute reports on Rehoboam and Jeroboam. Briefly overview the material in "Studying the Bible" for 1 Kings 12:1–19 to establish the background.

October 18, 1998

The Division of the United Kingdom

	Southern Kingdom	Northern Kingdom
King:	Rehoboam	Jeroboam
Capital:	Jerusalem	Shechem (later Samaria)
Name:	Judah	Israel
King's sin:	Insensitivity to people's needs	Built two gold calves and changed feast

Ask someone to read 12:25. Ask members the following questions and write the answers on the chart: Who was the king of Judah who caused the division? (Rehoboam.) (Call for the report on Rehoboam.) Who was the king of Israel? (Jeroboam.) (Call for the report on Jeroboam.) What were the capital cities of the two kingdoms? (Jerusalem, Shechem, and later Samaria.) On a large map, locate Jerusalem and Shechem. Ask: What was Rehoboam's sin? (Insensitivity to the needs of the people for tax relief.) What was Jeroboam's sin? (Built golden calves and ordained priests so people would worship in Israel and not go to Jerusalem; changed the date of the Feast of Tabernacles. Also see the list of four reasons in "Studying the Bible.") On the map, locate Bethel and Dan.

Give the Truth a Personal Focus

Ask, What role did selfishness play in Rehoboam's refusal to grant relief to the Israelites? (He was too selfish to listen to his older advisers. He wanted the power and wealth from Israel.) What role did selfishness play in Jeroboam's setting up of the golden calves and establishing the new places of worship? (He wanted to keep people from returning to Jerusalem to worship for fear they would start following Rehoboam again.) In the final analysis, how are these two sins similar? different?

Ask: How have you justified some sin to satisfy your selfish desires? What effects has this had on your life? How has it affected your relationship with God? with others?

Ask: What can you do to reunite the "divided" kingdom in your life? Close in prayer that all will be able to follow God's will for their lives and not follow their own selfish desires.

---

1. *The Great American Bathroom Book*, Vol. III (Salt Lake City: Compact Classics, 1994), 329.

The Work of Prophets

October 25 1998

Background Passage: 2 Kings 5:1–19
Focal Passages: 2 Kings 5:2–6, 9–14

During the periods of the united kingdom and the divided kingdom, the work of prophets came to the forefront. The usual Hebrew word for "prophet" seems to mean "one who speaks." True prophets spoke for God. Samuel spoke for God during Saul's reign; and Nathan spoke during the reign of David (2 Sam. 12:25). Elijah spoke for God during the dark days of Ahab's reign (1 Kings 17:1), and the Lord told Elijah to anoint Elisha as his successor (1 Kings 19:17–21). This lesson focuses on one of the most famous miracles of Elisha—the healing of Naaman.

▶**Study Aim:** *To describe the crucial roles played by the little maid, Elisha, Naaman, and Naaman's servants.*

STUDYING THE BIBLE

OUTLINE AND SUMMARY

I. Testifying about a Prophet (2 Kings 5:1–7)
  1. A little maid's testimony (5:1–4)
  2. A king's letter (5:5–7)
II. Responding to a Prophet's Word (2 Kings 5:8–14)
  1. Elisha's response to Naaman (5:8–10)
  2. Naaman's initial reaction (5:11–12)
  3. Naaman's cleansing (5:13–14)
III. Professing Faith to a Prophet (2 Kings 5:15–19)
  1. Naaman's faith and gratitude (5:15–16)
  2. Naaman's unusual request (5:17–19)

An Israelite slave girl's testimony was crucial in the healing of Naaman's leprosy (5:1–4). The king of Syria wrote the king of Israel, asking that Naaman be healed (5:5–7). When Naaman finally got to the house of Elisha, the prophet sent instructions about how to be healed by dipping in the Jordan (5:8–10). Naaman was so angry about what Elisha did that he left and headed home (5:11–12). The courageous question of his servants caused Naaman to obey the prophet; and when he did, he was healed (5:13–14). Naaman returned to Elisha, professed his faith, and unsuccessfully tried to get Elisha to accept gifts (5:15–16). He promised to worship only the Lord, but he asked for some dirt from Israel and for permission to accompany the king when he went to a pagan temple (5:17–19).

I. Testifying about a Prophet (2 Kings 5:1–7)

1. A little maid's testimony (5:1–4)

Verse 1 introduces us to Naaman [NAY uh muhn] and to his greatness and plight. He had many accomplishments: commander of the Syrian army, his king's favorite, winner of victories (with the Lord's help), and

October 25, 1998

a strong and courageous man. Yet he was stricken with the dread disease of leprosy.

2 And the Syrians had gone out by companies, and had brought away captive out of the land of Israel a little maid; and she waited on Naaman's wife.

3 And she said unto her mistress, Would God my lord were with the prophet that is in Samaria! for he would recover him of his leprosy.

4 And one went in, and told his lord, saying, Thus and thus said the maid that is of the land of Israel.

This incident took place during the period of the divided kingdom. The date of Elisha's death is placed about 800 B.C., and this took place late in Elisha's life. During the period of Elisha, the Northern Kingdom's main enemy was Syria (see 1 Kings 20; 22; 2 Kings 5–8). During a raid, the Syrians captured a girl who became a servant of the wife of Naaman.

The girl mentioned Samaria [suh MER ih uh]. This was the capital of Israel. Omri moved the capital there (1 Kings 16:24) after Jeroboam had first established it in Shechem.

This young girl had every reason to hate the Syrians who had taken her from home and family and made her a servant. However, she showed compassion for the plight of Naaman by seeking to help him be cured of his leprosy. She also showed great faith in the Lord and in the Lord's spokesman Elisha. In addition, she displayed courage in daring to speak as she did to her mistress. If her advice had led to a dead end, she could have been held responsible.

Verse 4 tells how word of her testimony reached the king of Syria. Some translations do not name the one who told the king. However, many translations say that Naaman himself heard of this (no doubt from his wife) and told the king of Syria. Thus, a number of people were involved in the chain of circumstances that sent Naaman to Elisha, but the young girl's testimony was the key.

2. A king's letter (5:5–7)

5 And the king of Syria said, Go to, go, and I will send a letter unto the king of Israel. And he departed, and took with him ten talents of silver, and six thousand pieces of gold, and ten changes of raiment.

6 And he brought the letter to the king of Israel, saying, Now when this letter is come unto thee, behold, I have therewith sent Naaman my servant to thee, that thou mayest recover him of his leprosy.

The king of Syria sent a letter for Naaman to take to the king of Israel. Naaman also took with him great amounts of silver and gold as well as many valuable clothes. This amounted to a fortune in that day.

When Naaman arrived in Samaria, he went to the king's palace and delivered the letter from the king of Syria. The tone of the letter sounds like an order. It also sounds as if the king of Israel himself was supposed to perform this miracle. Verse 7 shows that this was how the king of Israel interpreted the letter. He tore his clothes in grief. He knew he had no power to perform such a miracle. He suspected that the king of Syria was trying to create an excuse to attack Israel.

We cannot know what was in the mind of the king of Syria. He may have purposely worded the letter as if the king of Israel himself was to perform the miracle. On the other hand, the maid had said that the prophet was in Samaria; and the king of Syria probably assumed that the prophet either lived in the palace of the king or that the king knew of his power to heal.

II. Responding to a Prophet's Word (2 Kings 5:8–14)

1. Elisha's response to Naaman (5:8–10)

> 9 So Naaman came with his horses and with his chariot, and stood at the door of the house of Elisha.
>
> 10 And Elisha sent a messenger unto him, saying, Go and wash in Jordan seven times, and thy flesh shall come again to thee, and thou shalt be clean.

Chapter 5 does not give the name of the king of Israel, but it was probably Jehoram [jih HOH ruhm]. He was a son of Ahab, who lived much like his father had (2 Kings 3:1–3). Elisha had nothing but disdain for Jehoram. On one occasion, Elisha had helped the combined armies of Israel and Judah to defeat the Moabites; but Elisha made clear that he did this for the sake of Jehoshaphat [jih HAHSH uh fat], king of Judah, not for Jehoram. Elisha taunted Jehoram that he should have sought help from the false prophets of his father and mother (Jezebel; 2 Kings 3:6–27). Therefore, it is not surprising that Jehoram did not think of Elisha when Naaman showed up at his court.

When Elisha heard what had happened, he told the king to send Naaman to him. Both Naaman and everyone else—including the king of Israel—would learn that there was a prophet in Israel (5:8).

We don't know exactly where Elisha's house was. It was probably in or near Samaria. However, we can be reasonably sure that the prophet's house was much less imposing than the king's palace. Visualize the picture painted in verse 9. Imagine Naaman in his chariot. With him are all his servants and all the animals loaded with the presents he had brought.

Elisha didn't even come out to greet the great visitor from the north. He simply sent his servant with a message for Naaman. The message was simple and straightforward. Elisha's proposed cure for Naaman's leprosy was for the great general to dip himself seven times in the Jordan River. The prophet's message promised that when Naaman did this, his flesh would become as it had been before he got leprosy; and he would be cleansed.

2. Naaman's initial reaction (5:11–12)

> 11 But Naaman was wroth, and went away, and said, Behold, I thought, He will surely come out to me, and stand, and call on the name of the LORD his God, and strike his hand over the place, and recover the leper.

October 25, 1998

12 Are not Abana and Pharpar, rivers of Damascus, better than all the waters of Israel? may I not wash in them, and be clean? So he turned and went away in a rage.

Naaman was probably about out of patience by the time he found the prophet's modest home. He was not impressed by the runaround the king had given him, and he was even less impressed with this prophet's response. The Bible uses two words to describe how angry Naaman was: "wroth" and "rage." He was angry for three reasons:

1. Naaman had expected Elisha himself to come out. Instead, Elisha sent his servant. That seemed to Naaman a sign of disrespect or unconcern or both. Perhaps it also meant that the prophet knew he couldn't really help the leper. Naaman was so angry that he turned his chariot and left the house of Elisha behind.
2. Naaman had expected some dramatic display by the prophet in seeking to cure him. The Syrian thought that the prophet would stand, call on the name of his God, and strike his hand.
3. Naaman was also peeved at the advice about washing in the Jordan River. In his wars and travels, he had no doubt become familiar with the Jordan. Damascus was an ancient oasis that served and still serves as the capital of Syria. He saw no comparison of the Jordan to the Abana [AB uh nuh] and Pharpar [FAHR pahr] Rivers of his own country.

3. Naaman's cleansing (5:13–14)

13 And his servants came near, and spake unto him, and said, My father, if the prophet had bid thee do some great thing, wouldest thou not have done it? how much rather then, when he saith to thee, Wash, and be clean?

14 Then went he down, and dipped himself seven times in Jordan, according to the saying of the man of God: and his flesh came again like unto the flesh of a little child, and he was clean.

Naamam's servants helped him find healing. The little maid's testimony had sent him to Israel, and his servants' advice in verse 13 caused Naaman to obey the prophet's word. What they did took courage! They must have cared a lot for their master to take such a risk as to approach him when he was angry. In their opinion, Naaman was acting irrationally because of his hurt pride. They dared not say this to him directly. Instead, they asked him a question.

Naaman may have had time to cool off some by the time they spoke to him. At any rate, the general realized they were right. If Elisha had asked Naaman to do some difficult thing before healing him, Naaman would have tried almost anything. Instead the prophet asked him to do something simple: To wash in the Jordan River.

At last, Naaman dipped himself seven times in the Jordan—as Elisha had told him to do. What joy he must have felt when he came up the seventh time with his flesh as smooth as that of a child! What joy and relief his servants must have felt! Perhaps Elisha's strategy had been to test the humility and trust of the Syrian general. When he humbled himself and obeyed the prophet's words, he was healed and cleansed.

III. Professing Faith to a Prophet (2 Kings 5:15–19)
1. Naaman's faith and gratitude (5:15–16)

Naaman returned to the house of Elisha. This time he got to see the prophet. The Syrian professed his faith in the God whose power had healed him. Naaman declared that Israel's God was the one true God. He tried unsuccessfully to give the valuable gifts to Elisha.

2. Naaman's unusual requests (5:17–19)

Naaman's request for the two loads of dirt has been interpreted by some to mean that he shared the superstition of many in that day that each nation's god was confined to its own land. Another explanation is that Naaman wanted the dirt as an aid to worshiping the Lord. He had already professed faith in the Lord as the one and only God, and he now pledged that he would offer no sacrifices except to the Lord. His second request was to be pardoned for going to the temple of the Syrian god with the king. This does not mean that Naaman was asking for permission to worship a false god. It means that he did not want to offend his master the king. Elisha told Naaman to go in peace.

SUMMARY OF BIBLE TRUTHS

1. God can use anybody's testimony to accomplish great things.
2. Proud people often reject the call to simple humility and trust.
3. Some people take risks to help those they care about.
4. Wise people eventually recognize and take good advice.
5. God helps those who respond in trust and obedience.

APPLYING THE BIBLE

1. The power of testimony. Consider the power of the voice of three women.

(1) *A Welsh woman.* Revival began in Wales in 1904 and spread throughout the British Isles and to other countries. This began when a teenaged girl named Florrie Evans stood to her feet during a testimony meeting and, with a tremor in her voice, said, "I love Jesus Christ with all my heart." Several students of the revival see her testimony as the beginning of what we know as the Welsh Revival.[1]

(2) *A Romanian woman.* One night in December 1989, according to eyewitnesses, Nickolai Ceausescu, the communist head of Romania, was addressing a huge crowd of people when, in a momentary lull, a woman in the crowd shouted out, "You're a liar." The crowd took up her chant. Soon the crowd became a mob and, that night, Ceausescu and his wife Elena were both arrested and executed.[2]

(3) *In Syria.* In our Bible study today, we see a slave girl giving her voice to truth and becoming the instrument of her master's healing and, hopefully, his salvation.

Where is it that you should lift up your voice, even if your voice is the only one so raised up?

October 25, 1998

2. Why did Naaman take soil with him? While visiting downtown London recently, I was moved by the powerful elegance of Trafalfar Square, a famous landmark and favorite tourist attraction. It is dominated by the famed Nelson Column, which is a memorial to the English naval hero Lord Horatio Nelson for his great victory at Trafalgar. Near that column is a statue that seems altogether out of place; it is of the American president George Washington. Washington, of course, was British, and a famous one at that. The guide told us an interesting thing: Loyalists demanded that Washington's statue be set on soil imported from America; they didn't want a man they considered to be a traitor standing on English soil! Naaman's strange request to take Israel's soil back to Syria, as our author says, was on a different basis: More than likely, he believed the ancient superstition that a god could function effectively only on the soil of the country that believed in him. (Obviously, since God made all the soil everywhere in the universe, He was not so restricted. And, obviously, no pagan god can function on any soil anywhere!)

3. Naaman's compelling virtue was that he overcame his pride.
- "We can easily forgive a child who is afraid of the dark; the real tragedy of life is when men are afraid of the light" (Plato).
- "A man who is to take a high place before his fellows must take a low place before his God" (Anonymous).
- "Nothing sets a person so much out of the devil's reach as humility" (Anonymous).
- The young preacher went up to the pulpit swelled with a terrific sense of self-importance. After a while, having failed in his sermon, he returned to his seat in a dejected spirit. An older and wiser brother whispered to him, "If you'd gone up like you came down, you'd have come down like you went up." (Of course, if he was a man of true humility, that fact would have manifested itself going up *and* coming down, no matter what happened in the pulpit.)
- And then there was the preacher who was so proud of his humility that he could strut sitting down!

Where is pride preventing you from having God's best? Where has His Spirit spoken to you about that lately? A pastor friend of mine, who said he had taken a little too much into his own hands, said he heard the Lord quietly say to him some time ago, "Excuse me; I think you're sitting in my seat!"

4. Risking for others. Our lesson commentary mentions that "some people take risks to help those they care about." Isn't it interesting how we hesitate to take risks? And how full the Bible is of that virtue? Make a list of seven Bible characters who took risks for those they cared for. Who is it in your community that your church ought to take risks for? For whom should you take risks? (Consider Prov. 31:8–9, "Open thy mouth for the dumb in the cause of all such as are appointed to destruction. Open thy mouth, judge righteously, and plead the cause of the poor and needy." Who are the "dumb" in your community? Who is "appointed to destruction?" Who are the "poor and needy?" Should you take up their cause?

TEACHING THE BIBLE

October 25, 1998

▶ *Main Idea:* Elisha's miracle let all Israel and Syria know of God's power.
▶ *Suggested Teaching Aim:* To lead adults to have courage to speak for God and to follow His teachings.

A TEACHING OUTLINE

The Work of the Prophet

1. *Testifying about a Prophet (2 Kings 5:1–7)*
2. *Responding to a Prophet's Word (2 Kings 5:8–14)*
3. *Professing Faith to a Prophet (2 Kings 5:15–19)*

Introduce the Bible Study

Use "The power of testimony," "1. A Welsh woman" in "Applying the Bible" to introduce the Bible study.

Search for Biblical Truth

On a chalkboard, write *Servant Girl*. Ask members to look at 2 Kings 5:2–4 and identify qualities the servant girl demonstrated. List these on the chalkboard. (Among others: Compassion for Naaman, faith in the Lord, courage to dare to speak to her mistress.)

DISCUSS: How can someone who does not have much standing in the community use his or her influence for Christ?

On the chalkboard, write *Naaman*. Ask members to look at 5:5–7 and to list all they can determine about Naaman. (Among others: Had leprosy, ranked high in Syrian government, desperate enough to listen to a servant girl, wealthy, limited faith.)

DISCUSS: Why do we often have to wait until we have no other options before we turn to the Lord?

On the chalkboard, write *Elisha*. Ask members to look at 5:8–10. Ask members to list what the text tells them about Elisha. (Among others: Lived near Samaria, not impressed by Naaman's importance, sought to emphasize the Lord's power and not his. Add additional comments to the list of *Naaman* that members suggest. (Persisted in finding Elisha's house.)

DISCUSS: How would you have handled the situation with Naaman if you had been Elisha?

Ask members to look at 5:11–14 and list additional information about Elisha and Naaman. (Elisha: His prescription was correct, he did not try to impress Naaman by his actions, may have tested Naaman's humility and trust; Naaman: Felt snubbed by Elisha's nonroyal treatment, angry, finally came to his senses and listened to his servants, followed Elisha's directions, was healed.)

DISCUSS: What blessing have you missed out on because God did not do things in the manner in which you thought He should? What

October 25, 1998

blessings have you received because you followed God's leading, which at the time may not have seemed logical or practical?

Briefly summarize the material in "Studying the Bible" for 2 Kings 5:15–19 to complete the biblical story.

Give the Truth a Personal Focus

Ask, Which character would you like to be if the drama portrayed in our Scripture passage could be reenacted? Would you like to be the *Servant Girl* who was able to point someone to God's healing power? Would you be *Naaman*—someone who needs healing from the leprosy of sin? Would you be *Elisha* who has the power to prescribe the remedy for sin-sick people?

Encourage members to exercise fully whatever role they chose. If they are to witness, do it faithfully; if they need healing, claim it immediately; if they would like to be Elisha, don't take glory for themselves but give it to God.

---

1. Quoted in J. Edwin Orr, *The Flaming Tongue* (Chicago: Moody Press, 1973), 3.
2. Pat Robertson, *The New World Order* (Dallas: Word Publishing Co., 1991), 134.

Courage to Speak for God

November 1 1998

Background Passage: Amos 6–7
Focal Passages: Amos 6:1; 7:7–15

Prophets like Nathan, Elijah, and Elisha are called nonwriting prophets because they left no writings that now constitute the books of the Prophets in the Bible. Amos is among the writing prophets since we have the book of Amos. He was one of four great eighth-century prophets. Amos and Hosea preached in Israel, and Isaiah and Micah preached in Judah. Amos was the earliest of these four. He was a true prophet who spoke with clarity and courage the word of the Lord.

▶**Study Aim:** *To describe the preaching of Amos and his confrontation with Amaziah.*

STUDYING THE BIBLE

OUTLINE AND SUMMARY
 I. Sure Judgment on the Complacent Rich (Amos 6:1–14)
    1. Sins of the complacent rich (6:1–7)
    2. Sure judgment (6:8–14)
 II. Visions of Mercy and Judgment (Amos 7:1–9)
    1. Visions of locusts and of fire (7:1–6)
    2. Vision of the plumb line (7:7–9)
 III. Confrontation with Amaziah (Amos 7:10–17)
    1. Amaziah's report to Jeroboam (7:10–11)
    2. Amaziah's order to Amos (7:12–13)
    3. Amos's reply to Amaziah (7:14–17)

Amos condemned the complacent rich who lived in luxury and exploited the poor (6:1–7). He predicted sure judgment on them (6:8–14). When Amos prayed for the Lord's forgiveness after seeing two visions of doom, the Lord withheld judgment (7:1–6). The vision of the plumb line showed that the Lord would no longer withhold judgment from the wayward people (7:7–9). Amaziah, priest at Bethel, reported to Jeroboam that Amos was conspiring against the king (7:10–11). Amaziah told Amos to flee from Bethel and do any future prophesying in his native Judah (7:12–13). Amos denied being a professional prophet but insisted he was in Israel because God called him to go there (7:14–17).

I. Sure Judgment on the Complacent Rich (Amos 6:1–14)

1. Sins of the complacent rich (6:1–7)

1 Woe to them that are at ease in Zion, and trust in
the mountain of Samaria, which are named chief of the
nations, to whom the house of Israel came!

November 1 1998

Amos preached during the long reigns of Jeroboam II of Israel and Uzziah [uh ZIGH uh] of Judah (Amos 1:1; 2 Kings 14:23–29). Each of these kings reigned about forty years and ended their reigns about the same time. In round numbers, Amos preached a little before 750 B.C. He was not a native of Israel, as Hosea was. Hosea either overlapped or came soon after Amos (Hos. 1:1). Amos was from Tekoa [tee KOH uh], a little village in Judah (1:1). By trade, Amos had been a herdsman and dresser of trees until the Lord called him to preach to Israel (Amos 7:14–15).

Those were years of prosperity and success for Israel. The power of Assyria had not yet become a threat. Under Jeroboam and Uzziah, the combined borders of Israel and Judah almost matched the boundaries during the days of Solomon. This prosperity produced some very wealthy people, who lived in luxury and exploited the many poor people of the land. These rich people were complacent because they trusted in their own might and strong defenses as bulwarks against an enemy.

Amos 6:1 is a famous denunciation against these complacent rich people. Amos included both Judah (represented by Zion) as well as Israel. Both Jerusalem and Samaria, the capital of Israel (1 Kings 16:24), were built on mountains that served as fortresses. Thus, the rich of Israel trusted "in the mountain of Samaria."

"Named chief of the nations" literally reads "marked men of the chief nation." These rich men considered themselves marked for wealth, power, and prestige. The rest of the people in the house of Israel looked to them as leaders of society. However, Amos repeatedly accused the rich of ignoring and exploiting the poor while they lived in luxury (Amos 2:6–8). They refused to think about a day of divine reckoning; yet their actions hastened the day of violence in the land (6:3).

Their luxurious living and unconcern for the needs of others is described in Amos 6:4–6. Their homes and furnishings were nothing but the best. So were their foods. They partied with music, much wine, and expensive ointments. Meanwhile, they were "not grieved for the affliction of Joseph." Two of the most important tribes of the Northern Kingdom—Ephraim [EE frih uhm] and Manasseh [muh NASS uh]—were descended from the two sons of Joseph. The rich had no concern for the common people's plight or for the long-range consequences of their sins on the nation as a whole.

Because they led the people in sin, these complacent rich would lead the way into captivity (6:7).

2. Sure judgment (6:8–14)

The certainty of judgment is seen in the oath taken by the Lord to judge these sinners and their places of false security (6:8). Amos described the horrors of the coming siege (6:9–10). Mansions and hovels would be destroyed (6:11) because the rich had turned justice into poison (6:12). Their empty pride in their military victories (6:13) would not protect them when another nation overran them (6:14). Samaria fell to the Assyrians in 722 B.C. (2 Kings 17).

II. Visions of Mercy and Judgment (Amos 7:1–9)
1. Visions of locusts and of fire (7:1–6)

Amos saw a vision of locusts ready to devour the crops. After watching in horror as they stripped the land bare, Amos prayed that the Lord would forgive the people because the people were small in the face of such a disaster. The Lord "repented for this" in the sense of changing what He was about to do (7:1–3). Amos saw a vision of fire destroy the land and again prayed for forgiveness for the people. Again the Lord withheld judgment (7:4–6). We usually picture Amos as an angry prophet of doom, but these two incidents show his compassion for the Israelites.

2. Vision of the plumb line (7:7–9)

7 Thus he shewed me: and behold, the LORD stood upon a wall made by a plumb line, with a plumb line in his hand.

8 And the LORD said unto me, Amos, what seest thou? And I said, A plumb line. Then said the LORD, Behold, I will set a plumb line in the midst of my people Israel: I will not again pass by them any more.

9 And the high places of Isaac shall be desolate, and the sanctuaries of Israel shall be laid waste; and I will rise against the house of Jeroboam with the sword.

In the third vision, Amos saw the Lord on a wall holding a plumb line. Apparently this was a wall erected using a plumb line to ensure that it would be straight. The Lord told Amos that He was going to hold a divine plumb line up in the midst of His people Israel. The Lord knew that the wall of national life being erected in Israel would not be straight when judged by the plumb line of divine standards. Because the people had so deviated from divine standards, the Lord would no longer withhold judgment. Because of this word from the Lord, Amos did not pray for forgiveness as he had after the first two visions.

The "high places" were sites of local worship, which were usually built on hills. The "sanctuaries" referred to the worship places established by Jeroboam I and maintained by later kings at Bethel and Dan. Amos predicted that they would be destroyed. Some prophets condemned these worship sites because they diverted attention from the central place of worship at Jerusalem or because they had become nests of idolatrous worship. Amos, however, gave the people the benefit of the doubt and assumed that many intended to worship the Lord at these places. What he condemned was their hypocrisy in going through the motions of worshiping the God of justice while at the same time committing such injustices against the poor (Amos 5:21–24; 8:4–6). Amos also predicted that the Lord would wield the sword of judgment against Israel and the ruling house of Jeroboam.

III. Confrontation with Amaziah (Amos 7:10–17)
1. Amaziah's report to Jeroboam (7:10–11)

10 Then Amaziah the priest of Bethel sent to Jeroboam king of Israel, saying, Amos hath conspired against thee in the

November 1, 1998

midst of the house of Israel: the land is not able to bear all his words.

11 For thus Amos saith, Jeroboam shall die by the sword, and Israel shall surely be led away captive out of their own land.

Most of the book of Amos contains the prophecies of Amos, but Amos 7:10–17 is a narrative of an event in the life of Amos. Amaziah [am uh ZIGH uh] was the chief priest at the place of worship in Bethel. Remember that Jeroboam I had set up this shrine and named its priests (1 Kings 12:26–33). Thus, Amaziah was the hired priest of the king. He, therefore, reported to Jeroboam II about his own perception of the dangers posed by the renegade prophet from Judah. Amaziah's appraisal was that the land could not endure the words of Amos.

Specifically, Amaziah reported that Amos was conspiring against Jeroboam. The priest quoted what he claimed Amos had said. Amaziah may have heard Amos say the last part of verse 9. Thus, Amaziah's quotation of Amos was a loose paraphrase. Amos did foretell judgment by sword against the house of Jeroboam, but Amos was not part of a political conspiracy.

2. Amaziah's order to Amos (7:12–13)

12 Also Amaziah said unto Amos, O thou seer, go, flee thee away into the land of Judah, and there eat bread, and prophesy there:

13 But prophesy not again any more at Bethel; for it is the king's chapel, and it is the king's court.

Amaziah called Amos a "seer," another name for a prophet (1 Sam. 9:9). When used of legitimate prophets, the word *prophet* emphasized his speaking; and the word *seer* emphasized his visions and insights. Amaziah may have used the latter word as a term of ridicule, charging that whatever Amos claimed to see were hallucinations. Or he may have conceded that Amos was a legitimate prophet. What Amaziah clearly believed was that Amos had no authority to declare his messages or visions at Bethel. Because this was the king's established sanctuary, it belonged to the king, who had assigned authority over it to Amaziah as priest.

Therefore, Amaziah told Amos to flee from Bethel and to return to his native land. If he wanted to prophesy, let him do it in the land of Judah. The reference to eating bread referred to the practice of the people providing some support for prophets, such as feeding them.

3. Amos's reply to Amaziah (7:14–17)

14 Then answered Amos, and said to Amaziah, I was no prophet, neither was I a prophet's son; but I was an herdman, and a gatherer of sycamore fruit:

15 And the LORD took me as I followed the flock, and the LORD said unto me, Go, prophesy unto my people Israel.

Amos did not deny that he was a prophet, but he strongly denied that he had been a professional prophet. Some kings had official prophets who were hired to tell the king what he wanted to hear. Ahab, for example, had a large group of court prophets (1 Kings 22:6–8). Amos clearly was not this type of prophet. "A prophet's son" refers to being a member of a group of prophets, not to having a prophet as a father. Some of these were legitimate groups of real prophets (1 Kings 20:35; 2 Kings 2:3–4; 4:1, 38). Amos, however, was not a member of such a group.

By vocation, he had been a herdsman and a dresser of sycamore trees in his native Judah. However, the Lord took him from tending the flock and called him to be a prophet to God's people in Israel. Amaziah and Amos clashed over religious authority. Who had the authority at Bethel? Amaziah claimed he had the authority because it was the king's sanctuary and the king had appointed Amaziah to serve as priest at Bethel. Amos claimed he had the authority to speak for God at Bethel because God had called and sent him there.

Verses 16–17 predicted God's sure judgment on Amaziah and his family.

SUMMARY OF BIBLE TRUTHS

1. Wealth is sinful when gained by exploiting or ignoring the poor or when resulting in self-indulgence and spiritual complacency.
2. God is merciful; but He may bring sure judgment on persistent, impenitent sin.
3. Beware of compromising God's truth and your own integrity for personal advantage.
4. Fulfill the calling you have received from God.

APPLYING THE BIBLE

1. A silent call to the ministry. I once was leading the "quiet time" at a youth retreat. About thirty minutes after having sent them away to such a setting, a boy came running up to me and said something like this: "Pastor, a wonderful thing has just happened. I have been thinking for some time about going into the ministry. I told the Lord a while ago that if I fell asleep during my quiet time, I would take that as a sign of His calling. Guess what? I was sound asleep in no time!"

2. Sin hurts innocent people. Amos preached about the judment of God on sin. The tragedy of sin's judgment is not that it falls upon the guilty, but that it affects the guilty and those close to the guilty. All of us pray, "Dear Lord, punish me if you must, but don't punish my loved ones because of my sin." Shakespeare put this prayer in the mouth of the sinful Duke of Clarence:

> O God! If my deep prayers cannot appease
> But thou wilt be aveng'd on my misdeeds,
> Yet execute thy wrath in me alone,
> O, spare my guiltless wife and my poor children![1]

That prayer never has been answered, and it never will be. God cannot answer it! Let him who sins beware! That fact is a substantive part of Amos's message to the leaders of Israel.

November 1 1998

3. Judgments of the Lord. Amos could have said, in his promise of the righteous judgment of God, what Lincoln said in his second inaugural address: "Fondly do we hope, fervently do we pray, that this mighty scourge of war may speedily pass away. Yet, if God will that it continue until all the wealth piled by the bondsmen's two hundred and fifty years of unrequited toil shall be sunk, and until every drop of blood drawn with the lash shall be paid by another drawn with the sword, as was said three thousand years ago, so still it must be said, 'the judgments of the Lord are true and righteous altogether.'"

4. Truth is sometimes painful. Amos, at all costs and with a proper motive, under the impulsion of the Holy Spirit, spoke God's truth, though painful, to God's people.

- A recent book has this title: *I'm So Glad You Told Me What I Didn't Want to Hear.*[2]

- "I will not leave you temporarily happy at the risk of leaving you permanently sad."

- "You shall know the truth, and the truth shall make you mad" (Aldous Huxley).

- "Am I therefore become your enemy, because I tell you the truth?" (The Apostle Paul in Gal. 4:16).

Recall some painful truth—but redemptive truth—you have been told. (Remember that the Bible says, "Faithful are the wounds of a friend; but the kisses of an enemy are deceitful" (Prov. 27:6).

5. The 5 percent solution. I was once rebuked, rather sternly, by a church member. I went to prayer about the matter and was telling the Lord that about 98 percent of what had been said was wrong. (I felt I had to inform the Lord about the matter!) He gently said to my spirit, something like this, "Actually, the figure is more like 95 percent." I was about to engage in a moving self-congratulatory speech until I heard Him continue, "Now, what about the other 5 percent? She was right about that, you know. I know it's painful, but would you rather be a chastened man or a pampered boy?" I determined, before I finished that conversation with the Lord to benefit by the 5 percent! (Understand, of course, that the Lord and I agreed I was about 95 percent right—only on that specific issue!) List several painful truths that you think your pastor and your church must enunciate to the world around you.

TEACHING THE BIBLE

- *Main Idea:* God's judgment on Israel can warn people not to compromise their integrity but to fulfill God's calling.

- *Suggested Teaching Aim:* To lead adults to identify areas in which they may have compromised their integrity but are now willing to affirm God's will in their life.

A TEACHING OUTLINE

Courage to Speak for God

1. Sure Judgment on the Complacent Rich (Amos 6:1–14)
2. Visions of Mercy and Judgment (Amos 7:1–9)
3. Confrontation with Amaziah (Amos 7:10–17)

November 1 1998

Introduce the Bible Study

Use "Judgments of the Lord" in "Applying the Bible" to introduce the Bible study. Point out that God promised Israel that He would exact payment for Israel's mistreatment of the poor.

Search for Biblical Truth

IN ADVANCE, hang a plumb line near the front of the room where it can be seen. (Or draw one on a large sheet of paper.) Copy the seven summary statements from "Outline and Summary" and give them to seven members. Ask them to read them aloud at this time to summarize the background for the study.

On a chalkboard write, *What do we know about Amos?* Ask members to suggest what they know about Amos and write their statements on the chalkboard. Be sure the following are included: Prophesied in Israel about 750 B.C.; Israel fell to the Syrians in 721; he was Judean; not a professional prophet; ministered during a period of great prosperity in Israel; prophesied in Bethel, one of the cities where Jeroboam had set up a golden calf.

On a map, locate Bethel in Israel and Tekoa—Amos's home-town—in Judah.

Ask members to look at Amos 6:1–4 to find Amos's (and God's) basic charge against Israel. (Leaders were complacent and corrupt.)

Briefly summarize 7:1–6 and the vision of the locusts and of fire. Point out that in both of these cases, Amos pleaded for God to withhold judgment on Israel, and God granted his plea.

Point to the plumb line and say: The third vision Amos had was of a plumb line. Ask if anyone can explain how plumb lines are used. (To see if a wall or building is straight vertically.) Ask members to suggest ways Israel was "out of plumb" with God's divine commands. (Primarily: Abused the poor but many other reasons.)

Ask members to look at Amos 7:10–11. Briefly explain who Amaziah was. Ask: Of what did Amaziah accuse Amos? (Treason.) Why was what Amos said not treasonous? (The country could be saved only if it did what Amos suggested. He was the true patriot.)

Ask members to look at 7:14–15 and, using the material in "Study the Bible," identify what Amos meant by each of the titles with which he referred to himself.

To summarize this lesson on Amos, read the four truths in "Summary of Bible Truths" in "Studying the Bible."

November 1, 1998

Give the Truth a Personal Focus

Refer to the plumb line. Ask: If God were using this plumb line to measure you, how well would you come out? Are there areas of your life that do not measure up to God's divine plan? What makes you think you will come out any better than Israel did? In what areas are you willing to affirm God's will for your life?

Give members time to consider your questions, then close with a prayer that all will be willing to affirm God's will for their lives.

---

1. William Shakespeare, *King Richard III*.1.iv.
2. Barbara Johnson, *I'm Glad You Told Me What I Didn't Want to Hear* (Dallas: Word, 1996).

Writers of Songs

November 8 1998

Background Passage: Psalm 73
Focal Passages: Psalm 73:1–3,12–13,16–18, 21–26

A survey of the Old Testament deals not only with periods of history but also with kinds of literature. We have studied selections from law, history, and prophets. In this lesson, we study Psalm 73, from one of the books of poetry. The Psalms are a collection of hymns. Like our hymnals, the Psalms include a variety: Praise, confession, testimony, petition, and instruction.

▶**Study Aim:** *To describe how the psalmist's doubts arose and how they were resolved.*

STUDYING THE BIBLE

OUTLINE AND SUMMARY

I. Seeing Is Believing (Ps. 73:1–14)
   1. Believers sometimes have doubts (73:1–2)
   2. Why do the wicked prosper? (73:3–12)
   3. Why should I struggle to do right? (73:13–14)
II. Believing Is Seeing (Ps. 73:15–28)
   1. Handle your doubts wisely (73:15–17)
   2. Don't envy the wicked (73:18–22)
   3. God is with me (73:23–28)

The psalmist believed in the goodness of God, but he came close to falling into doubt (73:1–2). He envied the wicked who seemed to be healthy and prosperous (73:3–12). His struggles to do right seemed to be in vain because he faced troubles daily (73:13–14). Unable to find answers, he received insight while in the sanctuary of God (73:15–17). When he realized that the wicked were headed for destruction, he confessed that he had acted foolishly (73:18–22). He realized that God was with Him, held him safely, and would guide him in life and beyond death itself (73:23–28).

I. Seeing Is Believing (Ps. 73:1–14)

1. Believers sometimes have doubts (73:1–2)

> 1 Truly God is good to Israel, even to such as are of a clean heart.
>
> 2 But as for me, my feet were almost gone; my steps had well nigh slipped.

Verse 1 expresses the basic faith that the psalmist had been taught and had believed before his struggle with doubts. It is also the faith he reaffirmed with even greater conviction after the experiences described in the psalm.

God is good; but as for the psalmist, for a while he stumbled about until his feet almost came out from under him and almost caused him to fall. The people of faith in the Bible had questions and doubts that they

November 8, 1998

shared honestly with the Lord. For example, consider Gideon (Judg. 6:13), Elijah (1 Kings 19:4), Job (Job 19:22), Habakkuk (Hab. 1:2), and John the Baptist (Luke 7:20).

2. Why do the wicked prosper? (73:3–12)

3 For I was envious at the foolish, when I saw the prosperity of the wicked.

As the psalmist observed what he could see, the outward appearance of things was that wicked people were prospering. This made him wonder about the goodness and justice of God. Why would a just God allow wicked people to prosper?

Verses 4–11 give a detailed picture of the seeming prosperity of the wicked. They lived healthy lives and died pain-free deaths (73:4). They were immune from the troubles that plagued the rest of us (73:5). They wore their arrogance like an expensive necklace and their violence like valuable garments (73:6). They were well fed and wealthy all their days (73:7). They bragged about their moral corruption and their exploitation of others (73:8). They boasted not only of their sins on earth, but they also spoke arrogantly against heaven (73:9). These evil but successful people were popular with the people, who hung on their every word (73:10).

These evil people boldly asked, "How doth God know?" and "Is there knowledge in the most High?" (73:11). In other words, they questioned whether God knew or cared about things on earth.

12 Behold, these are the ungodly, who prosper in the world; they increase in riches.

Verse 12 summarizes how the psalmist viewed the wicked, when judged by outward appearances through self-pitying eyes. The word translated "prosper" means "safe" or "at ease." These wicked people lived wealthy, carefree lives—or so it seemed to the psalmist.

3. Why should I struggle to do right? (73:13–14)

13 Verily I have cleansed my heart in vain, and washed my hands in innocency.

Not only was the psalmist struggling with the seeming reality of the prosperity of the wicked, but he also was struggling with the contrast between their wealth and health and his poverty and troubles. The questions often are asked together: "Why do the wicked prosper and the righteous suffer?" This question becomes more than academic when a person of faith and righteousness experiences personal suffering or hard times. This causes the seeming prosperity of the ungodly wicked to stand out even more.

The psalmist mentioned his personal troubles in verse 14. We don't know exactly what he was going through, but he felt that he was plagued every day and rose each morning to be chastened. Therefore, he felt that he had cleansed his heart in vain. Why struggle to do the right thing if God is so unkind or unjust as to let a good man suffer while allowing the wicked to prosper?

II. Believing Is Seeing (Ps. 73:15–28)
1. Handle your doubts wisely (73:15–17)

> 16 When I thought to know this, it was too painful for me.
> 17 Until I went into the sanctuary of God; then understood I their end.

The psalmist took his questions to God. He realized that spreading his doubts among others would not have been the right thing to do (73:15).

After trying his best to find a satisfying answer to his dilemma by reasoning and thinking about it, he reached the conclusion that this was a dead-end street. Some questions have no easy answers. God seldom gives us an intellectual solution to our doubts (73:16).

Finally, the psalmist sought help by going into the sanctuary of God. In the place of worship, he found insight that helped to recover his spiritual balance. The word translated "understood" does not mean intellectual understanding so much as moral and spiritual insight. He was enabled to see reality through the eyes of faith. His perception of the wicked was corrected (73:18–22), and his perception of himself and of God was clarified (73:23–28).

Some people say, "Seeing is believing." That is, they say that faith is based on the kind of reality we can see, touch, and count. This was how the wicked viewed life all the time; and for a time, this was how the psalmist was looking at things. Then in the sanctuary, he rediscovered the truth that believing is seeing (Heb. 11:1). Faith opens the eyes of our spirits to see reality from God's perspective.

2. Don't envy the wicked (73:18–22)

> 18 Surely thou didst set them in slippery places: thou castedst them down into destruction.

As verse 17 says, he saw "their end." By looking at reality from God's perspective, he was lifted above the tangled wilderness of earthly life and given a vision of reality from the perspective of the eternal God. He realized that the prosperity of wicked people was superficial and temporary. God had placed them on a slippery slope, and they were sliding toward destruction. Disaster often overtook them in a moment (73:19).

> 21 Thus my heart was grieved, and I was pricked in my reins.
> 22 So foolish was I, and ignorant: I was as a beast before thee.

The prosperity of the wicked was like a dream or illusion (73:20). The psalmist was awakened from this dream to see that the wicked were not to be envied at all. This caused him to be convicted within his heart. He realized what a fool he had been to envy these people or to complain about his own troubles when he had so much for which to be grateful.

Notice the words *before thee*. This reminds us that the psalm was a prayer. He confessed to God that he had acted more like an animal than someone created in God's image.

3. God is with me (73:23–28)

> 23 Nevertheless I am continually with thee: thou hast holden me by my right hand.
> 24 Thou shalt guide me with thy counsel, and afterward receive me to glory.

November 8, 1998

25 Whom have I in heaven but thee? and there is none upon earth that I desire beside thee.

26 My flesh and my heart faileth: but God is the strength of my heart, and my portion for ever.

The words *nevertheless I* begin the psalmist's description of the blessings he had as a person of faith. He was contrasting himself not only with the wicked but also with his own perception of himself during his time of self-pity and doubt. Like the prodigal son, the psalmist "came to himself" (Luke 15:17). The psalmist was like someone awakening from a dream or being released from the illusion of some evil spell. He awoke to who he was and what he had in his relationship with God.

He realized that God had not forgotten or forsaken him. He was continually with God. God had been with him during the dark days of his questions and doubts. God held the psalmist in his strong right hand, even when the psalmist's faith was at its weakest. This underscores a great truth about true faith: *Faith is trust that God has a stronger hold on us than we have on Him.* The emphasis in the Bible is not on our great, unwavering faith as the basis for our security. The emphasis is on the grace and power of God who holds us at all times. Sometimes our faith is strong and sometimes it is weak; however, God's hold on us never slackens (John 10:27–29).

A second truth about faith is stated in verse 24: *Faith is trust that God will guide us through this life and through death itself.* The word translated "guide" in verse 24 is the same word translated "leadeth" in Psalm 23:3. As we face an uncertain future, we can trust the one who has led us in the past. He will lead us even through the valley of the shadow of death by His sustaining presence. In fact, He will lead us beyond that valley and death itself.

The ancient Hebrews did not have a fully developed view of life after death. God gradually revealed this precious doctrine to the full certainty based on Christ's resurrection from the dead. The psalmist made an important leap of faith when he affirmed that God would afterward receive him to glory. He asked himself this question: If I have fellowship with the eternal God, will that fellowship not extend beyond death into eternity?

A third truth about faith is in verse 25: *Faith is basically a relationship with God that is more valuable than anything else.* The psalmist had been foolish to envy the wicked for their wealth and to complain about his troubles, for he had the ultimate treasure in his relationship with God. He realized that he desired nothing beside God. He had discovered what Jesus taught in the parables of the hidden treasure and the pearl of great price (Matt. 13:44–46). When Paul was comparing his old life with his new life in Christ, he testified that everything he had once counted as an asset amounted to nothing when compared with what he had found in Jesus Christ (Phil. 3:7–9).

A fourth truth is in verse 26: *We are weak, but God is strong.* This implies Paul's discovery that when he was weak, then he was strong (2 Cor. 12:9–10). When we trust in our own wisdom and strength, we are weaker than we know. When we recognize our weakness and trust God's wisdom and strength, then we are strong because He is strong within us.

Verses 27–28 summarize the psalmist's conclusions: People who live in sins will perish; therefore, they are not to be envied but pitied (73:27). God's goodness is apparent when we draw near and trust in Him (73:28).

FOUR TRUTHS ABOUT FAITH

1. Faith is trust that God has a stronger hold on us than we have on Him.
2. Faith is trust that God will guide us through life and death.
3. Faith is a relationship with God that is life's greatest treasure.
4. Faith is based on the fact that we are weak but God is strong.

SUMMARY OF BIBLE TRUTHS

1. Faith is tested in the crucible of life's experiences.
2. People of faith take their doubts and questions to God.
3. God seldom explains "why," but He leads believers to a deeper trust.

APPLYING THE BIBLE

1. Heart answers. One of my daughters, when she was about five years old, was a bit under the weather. She crawled into my lap late one evening and said, plaintively, "Daddy, what's wrong with me?" I said something like, "Honey, I don't know, but it's going to be OK and I'm going to be here to take care of you." She went off to sleep immediately. I gave her an answer for her heart and not her head—but it was enough! I have, through the years, often thought our Lord does much the same for us in our quandaries.

2. Resolving our doubts in church. Note that the psalmist's problem was solved when he went to church. And remember Thomas's beautiful experience of resolving his doubt in precisely the same way. In John 20:24–31, we have that story recorded. Verse 24 makes it clear that Thomas was not in church (on a Sunday, by the way), and verse 26 makes it clear that he was in attendance on the following Sunday. That means he was honest about his doubt and made an effort to solve it.

3. Not all doubt is sincere. Hear this: The credibility of one's doubt may always be measured by the intensity with which he seeks to allay it! I once heard a young man of about thirty years old orating to some of his fellow workers in a medical lab about how he didn't believe the first chapter of Genesis. I had happened to walk in during his passionate discourse. He called for questions, and I gently asked him how many books he had read on Genesis, rounded off to the nearest ten. He had to admit that, in fact, he had never read one!

4. Doubts and difficulties. John Henry Newman said that "ten thousand difficulties do not make a doubt. A doubt is existential. A difficulty is intellectual, something you don't understand."[1] Now, that is a very important distinction. Every evidence is that the psalmist did not doubt God in any evil way, that is, his doubt was not "existential"; his problem was that he didn't understand. His difficulty was intellectual. Perhaps that is why God was so quick to give him the answer to his question.

5. Don't give up searching for the Lord. I remember witnessing to a woman of perhaps fifty years of age, and she said to me that she had not given God a thought since she was about twelve. At that age, she

November 8 1998

said, she gave up on the entire matter of religion. I encouraged her to reopen the investigation, and observed that, at that age, a lot of youngsters believe the moon is cheese. It would be a tragic thing to give up one's search into the ultimate nature and meaning of the entire universe at twelve. Or fifty plus twelve! How would you counsel doubters you know to reopen their investigation of religion, specifically, the Christian faith. Remember Hosea's wonderful promise: "Then shall we know, if we follow on to know the LORD" (Hos. 6:3).

7. Think on the good things in life. A very interesting thing happened to me yesterday about the matter of doubt. A member of our church called me crying and saying that her husband (a church member of many years) had just announced to her that he could no longer believe in God. He said too many bad things had happened to him—things like his parents' dying (they were both in very advanced years), trouble with a child—and other things such as children being born with deformities. Is it not an interesting phenomenon that he (like most doubters) had nothing to say about the good things that had happened to him? If the bad is hard to explain, what about the good? He is in great health, great wealth, has a beautiful and loving family, a host of devoted friends, not to mention the fact that he was born and reared in the lap of plenty in America! Of course he, like the psalmist, and all the rest of us, has questions. That is part and parcel of the human condition. But he, like all of us, should confess with Mark Twain: "It is not what I don't understand about the Bible that bothers me; it is what I do understand that bothers me!"

TEACHING THE BIBLE

- *Main Idea:* God does not always answer our doubts, but He does increase our faith if we will trust Him.
- *Suggested Teaching Aim:* To lead adults to trust in God when He doesn't answer their doubts.

A TEACHING OUTLINE

Writer of Songs

   I. *Seeing Is Believing (Ps. 73:1–14)*
      1. *Believers sometimes have doubts (73:1–2)*
      2. *Why do the wicked prosper? (73:2–12)*
      3. *Why should I struggle to do right? (72:13–14)*
  II. *Believing Is Seeing (Ps. 73:15–28)*
      1. *Handle your doubts wisely (73:15–17)*
      2. *Don't envy the wicked (73:18–22)*
      3. *God is with me (73:23–28)*

Introduce the Bible Study

Use "Heart answers" in "Applying the Bible" to introduce the lesson. Point out that God may not always give us the answers we need, but He does lead believers to a deeper trust.

On a chalkboard write, *Seeing is believing* and *Believing is seeing.* Ask, Which of these statements is true for believers? (Both can be; the second demonstrates more faith.)

Search for Biblical Truth

Ask, Have you ever doubted God's goodness to you? What caused you to doubt? Ask members to open their Bibles to Psalm 73:1–2. Ask, What is the basic statement of this psalm? (God's goodness.) Point out that the psalmist's questioning is done within the firm belief in God's basic goodness to him and the whole nation.

Ask, How does the psalmist describe his own spiritual condition? (Full of doubt, ready to fall.) Ask, Which of the following words describes the psalmist's condition: doubtful, envious, honest, trusting. (All may apply, although there was not much trust—yet he trusted God enough to bring his doubts to Him.)

Ask members to look at 73:3, 12. Ask, Does the fact that the wicked seemingly prosper while dedicated believers suffer bother you? Point out that it bothered the psalmist.

Ask, What is often the next step when someone thinks evil is being rewarded and good is going unrewarded? Point to the third subpoint on the outline. This was the psalmist's reaction, and it often is ours.

Call attention to the second section of the outline: *Believing Is Seeing.* Ask members to look at 73:16–17. Ask, What helped the psalmist put things into perspective? (Went to the temple and addressed God.) What did he come to understand? (Enabled to see reality through the eyes of faith; saw the wicked and himself clearly.)

Ask members to look at 73:18–22. Ask, What did the psalmist come to understand about the wicked? (They were about to fall.) To what did the psalmist compare his actions? (He had acted more like an animal than a person.)

IN ADVANCE, copy the four truths about faith mentioned in "Studying the Bible." Prepare a brief lecture in which you follow this pattern: (1) Place a statement strip on the wall. (2) Ask someone to read the corresponding Scripture passage. (3) Ask, Why do you agree or disagree with this statement? (4) Add anything from the material in "Studying the Bible" that will help members understand the statement.

Give the Truth a Personal Focus

Read the Main Idea of the lesson aloud: God does not always answer our doubts, but He does increase our faith if we will trust Him. Distribute paper and pencils and ask members to write their own psalm that expresses their doubts to God but also affirms their faith.

Allow as many as wish to read their psalms to do so, but do not force anyone to do so.

Close with prayer that God will increase our faith when we doubt.

---

1. Quoted in Roy Abraham Verghese, ed., *The Intellectuals Speak Out About God* (Chicago: Regnery Gateway, 1984), 180.

November 8 1998

November 15 1998

False Hopes and Judgment

Background Passages: Jeremiah 19; 21:1–10
Focal Passages: Jeremiah 19:1–4, 10–11; 21:1–2, 8–10

The Old Testament we use has the same thirty-nine books as the Hebrew Scriptures, but the sequence and divisions are different. The Hebrew divisions are Law, Prophets, and Writings; our divisions are Law, History, Poetry (Wisdom), and Prophets. We have two subdivisions for Prophets: the first five are called Major Prophets, and the other twelve are called Minor Prophets. The terms *major* and *minor* refer to length, not to importance. Thus, both Amos and Jeremiah were important prophets, but Jeremiah is called a Major Prophet because of the greater length of the book.

▶**Study Aim:** *To describe Judah's sins and false hopes and what Jeremiah said about each.*

STUDYING THE BIBLE

OUTLINE AND SUMMARY

I. Pronouncing Judgment on Sins (Jer. 19:1–15)
   1. The Lord's instructions to Jeremiah (19:1–2)
   2. The sins of Judah (19:3–9)
   3. A shattered nation (19:10–15)
II. Destroying False Hopes (Jer. 21:1–10)
   1. The false hopes (21:1–2)
   2. An unpopular message (21:3–7)
   3. A choice for the people (21:8–10)

KEY PEOPLE AND EVENTS SOUTHERN KINGDOM OF JUDAH	
Kingdom Divides	Rehoboam's refusal to listen to grievances of the northern tribes caused the kingdom to divide (1 Kings 12).
David's Line Continues	All the kings of Judah were descendants of David. Some were good, and some were evil.
Good King Hezekiah	When the Assyrians attacked Judah, the religious reformer King Hezekiah prayed; and the Lord promised through Isaiah to deliver Judah (2 Kings 18–20; 2 Chron. 29–32).
Evil King Manasseh	Hezekiah's evil son Manasseh sealed Judah's fate during his long, infamous reign (2 Kings 21:1–18; 2 Chron. 33:1–20).
Judah's Final Warning	Jeremiah delivered God's final warning to Judah. The warning was ignored, and the Babylonians destroyed Jerusalem in 587/86 B.C. (2 Kings 22:1–23:30; 2 Chron. 34–36).

November 15, 1998

The Lord told Jeremiah to take a bottle and go with some elders to a certain valley (19:1–2). The prophet was told to denounce the people for turning from the Lord to idolatry that involved human sacrifice (19:3–9). After breaking the bottle, Jeremiah declared that the Lord would shatter Judah and Jerusalem (19:10–15). King Zedekiah sent to Jeremiah, hoping that the Lord would deliver the people from the Babylonians (21:1–2). The Lord told him that God would fight not for them but against them (21:3–7). He offered the people a choice of surrendering and living or staying in Jerusalem and dying (21:8–10).

I. Pronouncing Judgment on Sins (Jer. 19:1–15)
1. The Lord's instructions to Jeremiah (19:1–2)

> 1 Thus saith the LORD, Go and get a potter's earthen bottle, and take of the ancients of the people, and of the ancients of the priests;
>
> 2 And go forth unto the valley of the son of Hinnom, which is by the entry of the east gate, and proclaim there the words that I shall tell thee.

Chapter 18 tells of Jeremiah's visiting a potter at work making a vessel of clay. In chapter 19, the prophet was told to get a completed work of a potter. The Hebrew word translated "bottle" referred to an artistic and expensive pitcher. The Lord also told Jeremiah to invite the elders of the people and the elder priests (see 2 Kings 19:2) to go with him.

Jeremiah 1:1–3 tells us that the prophet's long ministry began in the time of King Josiah and extended to the time of Zedekiah [zed uh KIGH uh], Judah's last king (2 Kings 23–25). As a young prophet, Jeremiah witnessed the failure of Josiah's attempt to reform Judah. Josiah was followed by four evil kings. One of these was Jehoiakim [jih HOY uh kim]. The events of Jeremiah 19 probably occurred during the early years of Jehoiakim.

Jeremiah was told to take the elders to the valley of the son of Hinnom [HIN ahm]. This valley was south of the ancient city, which later became Jerusalem (Josh. 15:18, 19).

2. The sins of Judah (19:3–9)

> 3 And say, Hear ye the word of the LORD, O kings of Judah, and inhabitants of Jerusalem; Thus saith the LORD of hosts, the God of Israel; Behold I will bring evil upon this place, the which whosoever heareth, his ears shall tingle.
>
> 4 Because they have forsaken me, and have estranged this place, and have burned incense in it unto other gods, whom neither they nor their fathers have known, nor the kings of Judah, and have filled this place with the blood of innocents.

Although Jeremiah took only the elders with him, his message was directed to all the kings and people of Judah and Jerusalem. The Northern Kingdom had been destroyed over a hundred years before. When Jeremiah spoke, only the kingdom of Judah with its capital at Jerusalem survived.

November 15 1998

The Lord told Jeremiah to speak His word to them. In those days, words were considered to be powerful extensions of the person who spoke them. This was true of human words; how much more of the word of "the LORD of hosts"! This is one of many titles for God. This title depicts the Lord as the leader of vast heavenly forces. His word thus goes forth with the power of this God (Isa. 55:10–11).

The Lord's judgments would be so terrible that the ears of those who heard of them would tingle (compare 1 Sam. 3:11; 2 Kings 21:12). The terrible judgments would match the terrible sins committed in the valley of the son of Hinnom. The basic sin, just as it is the universal human sin, was forsaking the Lord. Throughout their history, forsaking the Lord involved turning to idolatry. (Review the cycle of sin in Judges 2.)

Their sins were especially terrible in two ways: For one thing, they worshiped gods that their forefathers had not even known about. These were probably the gods of the Assyrians and Babylonians. However, the most terrible expression of their sin was shedding innocent blood. Verse 5 confirms that this was child sacrifice. Other references to the valley show that it was an ancient site for this unspeakable abomination (Jer. 7:31–32; 2 Kings 23:10; 2 Chron. 28:3). This sin had been practiced in Israel (2 Kings 16:3) and in Judah (2 Kings 17:17). This was one of the gross sins of Manasseh [muh NASS uh], whose long reign of evil sealed the doom of Judah (2 Kings 21:6, 10–16).

This valley, also called Tophet [toh fet], would be called the valley of slaughter (19:6). The birds and beasts would feast on the unburied bodies of those slain by the sword of an enemy whom God would send upon Judah (19:7). Jerusalem would become a place of scorn for other nations (19:8). During the enemy siege, conditions would become so desperate that some of the people would eat their own children (19:9).

3. A shattered nation (19:10–15)

> **10 Then shalt thou break the bottle in the sight of the men that go with thee,**
>
> **11 And shalt say unto them, Thus saith the LORD of hosts; Even so will I break this people and this city, as one breaketh a potter's vessel, that cannot be made whole again: and they shall bury them in Tophet, till there be no place to bury.**

The Lord told Jeremiah to break the bottle while the elders watched. The shattered bottle signified the shattering of the nation. Just as the bottle broke into pieces that could not be put back together, so would the nation of Judah be shattered. Verses 12–15 make clear that the judgment included not only Tophet but also the city of Jerusalem.

This kind of prophetic symbolism was used by many of the prophets. It consisted of two parts: (1) the symbol and (2) the verbal explanation. Jeremiah and Ezekiel especially are remembered for the use of prophetic symbolism. Here are passages containing some of Jeremiah's other symbols: 5:1–6; 13:1–11; 16:1–9; 25:15–29; 32:1–15.

Jeremiah's twin emphases were judgment and hope. He preached judgment until judgment fell; then he preached hope. The shattering of the bottle was obviously a symbol of the shattering of the nation. However, later symbols and messages offered long-range hope. These are not contradictory. The nation of Judah was doomed and destroyed; however, after the Exile, God began again with a faithful remnant of His people.

II. Destroying False Hopes (Jer. 21:1–10)
1. The false hopes (21:1–2)
> 1 The word which came unto Jeremiah from the LORD, when king Zedekiah sent unto him Pashur the son of Melchiah, and Zephaniah the son of Maaseiah the priest, saying,
> 2 Enquire, I pray thee, of the LORD for us; for Nebuchadrezzar king of Babylon maketh war against us; if so be that the LORD will deal with us according to all his wondrous works, that he may go up from us.

About twenty years passed between chapters 19 and 21. Zedekiah was the last king of Judah. The dominant world power in Jeremiah's day was Babylonia. After Babylonia defeated the mighty Assyrians, Judah became a subject state under the Babylonians. Babylonia's only real rival was Egypt. Judah was caught in the power struggle between these two powers. From time to time, a king of Judah would decide to rebel against Babylonian rule by allying with Egypt. The people of Judah always paid a terrible price for these alliances.

Zedekiah had made a fateful decision to rebel. The army of Babylon was about to lay siege to Jerusalem, in what became the final siege before the fall of Judah. The Babylonians were led by Nebuchadnezzar [neb yoo kad NEZZ ur] (sometimes spelled Nebuchadrezzar).

During that time, King Zedekiah sent word to Jeremiah. Zedekiah hoped that the prophet would tell him that the Lord would defend Jerusalem as He had in earlier times. Zedekiah was thinking especially of the Lord's deliverance of Jerusalem over a century before. After the Assyrians had destroyed the Northern Kingdom in 722 B.C., they swept into Judah determined to destroy Jerusalem. King Hezekiah [hez ih KIGH uh] prayed and asked the prophet Isaiah for a word from the Lord. Isaiah promised that the Lord would fight for Judah and drive away the Assyrians. The account of that victory is in Isaiah 36–37.

The political and religious leaders of later generations assumed that because the Lord delivered Jerusalem from the Assyrians, He would do the same for future generations. Based on this assumption, they proclaimed that God would never let Jerusalem be destroyed. Zedekiah's paid prophets had been assuring the king of this. Only Jeremiah called this a false hope. In a memorable sermon in the temple, Jeremiah condemned those who clung to the hope that the temple would stand forever (Jer. 7:7).

2. An unpopular message (21:3–7)
Jeremiah dashed Zedekiah's false hopes with his reply. The prophet said that the Lord would turn the Judeans' weapons of war against them (21:3–4). Not only would the Lord not fight for them, but the Lord would fight against them (21:5). Jeremiah often said that the Lord would use the Babylonians as His instruments of judgment on Judah. Here he went a step further by insisting that it was the Lord Himself who would smite

November 15, 1998

the city with the sword, famine, and pestilence (21:6). Then the Lord warned that He would deliver Zedekiah into the merciless hands of Nebuchadnezzar (21:7).

3. A choice for the people (21:8–10)

> 8 And unto this people thou shalt say, Thus saith the LORD; Behold, I set before you the way of life, and the way of death.
>
> 9 He that abideth in this city shall die by the sword, and by the famine, and by the pestilence: but he that goeth out, and falleth to the Chaldeans that besiege you, he shall live, and his life shall be unto him for a prey.
>
> 10 For I have set my face against this city for evil, and not for good, saith the LORD: it shall be given into the hand of the king of Babylon, and he shall burn it with fire.

Verses 8–10 were addressed to the common people. They still had a choice. Their decision would determine whether they lived or died in the siege and fall of Jerusalem. The people could stay inside the city and die in fighting or by famine or pestilence. Or they could go out to the enemy lines. They would be made captives, but at least they would live.

You can easily see why Jeremiah seemed like a traitor to many Judeans. He was advising the people not to fight to defend their city against the foreign invaders. Instead he was advising them to surrender.

Jeremiah's prophecies of doom came true. The siege began in 588 B.C. In 586, the fortress city of Jerusalem fell. After looting the houses and temple, the Babylonians burned the city. Zedekiah's attempt to escape failed. The king was forced to watch his sons be executed. Then his eyes were put out, and he was led in chains into Babylon (2 Kings 25:4–7).

SUMMARY OF BIBLE TRUTHS

1. Based on past divine mercy and blessings, some people think they and their nation are immune from divine judgment.
2. Persistent sin and impenitence will bring judgment on any person or nation.
3. Delivering a stern message of God's sure judgment subjects the speaker to ridicule and other forms of opposition.

APPLYING THE BIBLE

1. Say yes to God. A retired missionary told our church of his call to the ministry. He had been dodging the Lord for some time about the matter. One evening, tired of running, he hunkered down under a small tree after feeding cattle on an Oklahoma farm and said, "Lord, before you say it, the answer is 'Yes'." That "Yes" took him to a lifetime of intense service to the Lord and to His people. It makes us think of the lines of one of our favorite congregational songs:

> Yes, Lord, yes! to Your will and your Way
> Yes, Lord, yes! I will trust You and obey.

> When Your Spirit speaks to me, with my whole heart I'll agree
> And my answer will be yes, Lord, yes!

Israel would have missed national tragedy if she had sung that song—and meant it!

2. Courage to speak the truth. We honor Jeremiah and Amos because of their fearless preaching of the truth regardless of the consequences. A pastor told me of a preacher who had something of Amos and Jeremiah in him. It seems that he had witnessed several times to a state senator. The senator always ended those discussions with this litany: "No, thanks, preacher; my religion is in my wife's name; I don't need any." About three weeks after one such session, the state senator died, and the pastor was called on to direct his funeral service. The pastor's entire message was comprised of a short report of the aforementioned sessions and this concluding statement: "I have no reason to believe, upon investigation, that there has been any change in the matter. You are dismissed." The story created a furor in the small town, and there was an immediate move to fire the preacher. But a strange thing happened: The next Sunday morning, at the invitation, several men were saved, including an uncle of the man who told me that story. The town experienced a revival of interest in the things of God because someone dared—hopefully in grace—to speak the truth.

3. It is intriguing how every generation tends to refuse to heed the message of prophets, and then honors them after their death. Remember that our Lord said to the Pharisees, "Woe unto you! for ye build the sepulchres of the prophets, and your fathers killed them. Truly ye bear witness that ye allow the deeds of your fathers" (Luke 11:47–48). And recall that He also said, "A prophet is not without honor, save in his own country, and in his own house" (Matt. 13:57). Many believe Homer was the greatest of all Greek authors, yet:

> Seven wealthy towns contend for Homer dead,
> Through which the living Homer begged his bread.[1]

4. Some disturbing questions. Jeremiah's message centered in a warning of God's coming judgment. Consider these questions:
- Could America ever be judged by God?
- Is it possible that He is even now judging us?
- For what sins might He be judging us now or be planning to do so in the future?
- May we expect deliverance from God's righteous judgment because God has blessed us so abundantly in the past?
- How, precisely, would we know that God was judging us?
- Is there a means of escaping God's judgment and, if so, how?

5. Thoughts on popular preaching.
- Vance Havner once said, "There is no place on earth so slippery as the floor of a popular pulpit."
- Soren Kierkegaard once observed that preachers are often given the largest parishes not because they live the life of sacrifice which our

November 15, 1998

Lord did but because they are able to describe His sacrifice most eloquently.

▶ "For the time will come when they will not endure sound doctrine; but after their own lusts shall they heap to themselves teachers, having itching ears" (2 Tim. 4:3).

And let us consider the words of Theodore Storm:

> "One may ask, "What comes of it?"
> Another, "What is right?"
> And therein lies the difference
> Between the knave and the knight.

TEACHING THE BIBLE

▶ *Main Idea*: God pronounces judgment on all those who refuse to hear and obey His warnings.

▶ *Suggested Teaching Aim*: To lead adults to identify what they can do to avoid God's judgment on them.

A TEACHING OUTLINE

False Hopes and Judgment

I. Pronouncing Judgment on Sins (Jer. 19:1–15)
   1. The Lord's instructions to Jeremiah (19:1–2)
   2. The sins of Judah (19:3–9)
   3. A shattered nation (19:10–15)

II. Destroying False Hopes (Jer. 21:1–10)
   1. The false hopes (21:1–2)
   2. An unpopular message (21:3–7)
   3. A choice for the people (21:8–10)

Introduce the Bible Study

Ask members to list symbolism used in the Bible. Write these on a chalkboard. (For Christians, the Lord's Supper and baptism are two of the most significant.)

Point out that Jeremiah used symbolism to warn Judah of its fate.

Search for Biblical Truth

IN ADVANCE, write out the six summary statements in "Outline and Summary" and enlist two people to read them alternately to establish the background. **IN ADVANCE**, make two posters. On one poster write *Judgment*; on the other write *Hope*. Place the *Judgment* poster on the wall and say that Jeremiah's message had two parts. The first part was judgment. Ask members to open their Bibles to Jeremiah 19:1–2 and find what symbolism Jeremiah used. On a map of Jerusalem, locate Hinnom Valley. Explain (1) that the Hinnom Valley had been used as a place for child sacrifice; (2) chapter 19 probably occurred during the early years of King Jehoiakim (609–598 B.C).

Ask, According to 19:3–4, 10–11, what sins had Judah committed? (Worshiped foreign gods and offered child sacrifice.) What did God say He would do to the nation? (Shatter the nation.)

Point out that Jeremiah's first emphasis was judgment. Now place the second poster on the wall and say that he also emphasized hope.

Lecture briefly covering the following points: (1) the events of chapter 21 occurred about twenty years after the events of chapter 19; (2) Zedekiah, Judah's last king, was on the throne; (3) Babylonia was the most powerful nation in the world; (4) Zedekiah had rebelled against Babylonia and allied Judah with Egypt; (5) Nebuchadnezzar was preparing to lay siege to Jerusalem; (6) Zedekiah sent to Jeremiah and asked if there was any hope that God would deliver Judah as He had in the past.

Ask members to look at 21:8–10. Ask, What kind of hope did Jeremiah hold out? (If they surrendered to the Babylonians, they would live; if they refused, they would die.)

Give the Truth a Personal Focus

Read the following list of questions in No. 4, "Applying the Bible," and ask members to respond:
1. Could America ever be judged by God?
2. Is it possible that He is even now judging us?
3. For what sins might He be judging us now or be planning to do so in the future?
4. May we expect deliverance from God's righteous judgment because God has blessed us so abundantly in the past?
5. How precisely would we know that God was judging us?
6. Is there a means of escaping God's judgment and, if so, how?

Read the Main Idea: God pronounces judgment on all who refuse to hear and obey His warnings. Use the illustration in No. 2, "Applying the Bible" to close the lesson.

---

1. Anonymous quotation cited in *Bartlett's Familiar Quotations,* Eleventh Edition, pp. 123–124.

November 22 1998

God's Vision for Exiles

Background Passage: Ezekiel 37
Focal Passages: Ezekiel 37:1–11a, 25a, 26–27

The book of Ezekiel is a key source for the period of the Exile. Ezekiel was among the exiles carried to Babylon in 597 B.C. His call as a prophet came in 593 B.C. (Ezek. 1:1–3). Thus, his ministry overlapped the latter part of the ministry of Jeremiah. The prophets Ezekiel and Jeremiah had similar messages, although Jeremiah preached in Judah and Ezekiel preached to the exiles in Babylon. They both preached judgment before Jerusalem fell in 586 B.C. After that, Jeremiah and Ezekiel preached hope. Ezekiel 37 is among the most familiar of Ezekiel's passages about hope.

▶**Study Aim:** *To summarize the meaning of the vision of the dry bones and the sign of the two sticks.*

STUDYING THE BIBLE

OUTLINE AND SUMMARY

I. Vision of Valley of Dry Bones (Ezek. 37:1–14)
   1. Dry bones (37:1–3)
   2. Command to preach to the bones (37:4–6)
   3. The breath of life (37:7–10)
   4. Hope for hopeless Israel (37:11–14)
II. Sign of Two Sticks (Ezek. 37:15–28)
   1. Two sticks joined (37:15–19)
   2. Hope for the future (37:20–28)

God caused Ezekiel to see a valley of dry bones. He asked the prophet if the bones could live (37:1–3). God told Ezekiel to prophesy to the bones and that God would cause them to live (37:4–6). God's Spirit made the dry bones into living people (37:7–10). God used the vision to promise hope to the hopeless exiles (37:11–14). God led the prophet to use the symbol of two sticks joined (37:15–19). God promised a bright future for Israel (37:20–28).

I. Vision of Valley of Dry Bones (Ezek. 37:1–14)

1. Dry bones (37:1–3)

1 The hand of the LORD was upon me, and carried me out in the spirit of the LORD, and set me down in the midst of the valley which was full of bones,

2 And caused me to pass by them round about: and, behold, there were very many in the open valley: and, lo, they were very dry.

3 And he said unto me, Son of man, can these bones live? And I answered, O Lord God, thou knowest.

One of the characteristics of the book of Ezekiel is its visions (Ezek. 1:4–28; 10:1–22; 11:22–25). Ezekiel tells how he was carried by the Spirit to a valley full of bones. As he got a closer look at the bones, Ezekiel observed that they were "very many" and "very dry." The bones were in the open, showing that the bodies had not been buried. Their dryness showed that they had been there for a long time. The bones were not joined together as skeletons (see v. 7). Apparently the bones of the dead had been scattered by scavengers and by the weather. Based on what is said in verse 10 about an army, the bones apparently marked the site of a battle in which the dead had remained unburied.

As Ezekiel looked at this terrible sight, the Lord suddenly asked him, "Son of man, can these bones live?" From a human point of view, the answer was no. Yet Ezekiel was too wise to give such an answer to the Lord. The prophet knew the concern and power of God, and he knew that God could make the bones come alive—if He chose to do so.

Notice that the Lord called Ezekiel "son of man." This phrase is found ninety times in Ezekiel as a title for the prophet. Most Bible students understand this as a reminder of the prophet's humanity and frailty. This use is different from the use in Daniel 7:13–14, which became the basis for Jesus' use of this title for Himself.

2. Command to preach to the bones (37:4–6)

4 Again he said unto me, Prophesy upon these bones, and say unto them, O ye dry bones, hear the word of the LORD.

5 Thus saith the Lord God unto these bones; Behold, I will cause breath to enter into you, and ye shall live:

6 And I will lay sinews upon you, and will bring up flesh upon you, and cover you with skin, and put breath in you, and ye shall live; and ye shall know that I am the LORD.

The Lord commanded Ezekiel to prophesy to the dry bones. Most preachers would feel foolish preaching to dry bones, but Ezekiel had had much experience preaching to people who were as unresponsive as bones would be (Ezek. 2–3; 12:22–28; 33:30–33).

The word of the Lord to the bones promised new life. Through Ezekiel, God told the bones that they would live. He even described the process. God would put sinews and flesh on the bones; then He would put breath into them. As a result, the dry bones would live. Notice the emphasis on this as the work of the Lord. "I will" is repeated in verses 5 and 6. As a result of this miracle of new life for dry bones, the resurrected dead and the prophet would know that God is the Lord.

God would accomplish this miracle through His word. In the Bible, words meant more than they do today. Words were extensions of the speaker. Thus, the word of the Lord was one way of describing the Lord Himself at work through the agency of His word. No wonder Isaiah 55:10–11 says that the word of the Lord will accomplish the purpose for which it was sent forth.

3. The breath of life (37:7–10)

7 So I prophesied as I was commanded: and as I prophesied, there was a noise, and behold a shaking, and the bones came together, bone to his bone.

8 And when I beheld, lo, the sinews and the flesh came up upon them, and the skin covered them above: but there was no breath in them.

November 22, 1998

9 Then said he unto me, Prophesy unto the wind, prophesy, son of man, and say to the wind, Thus saith the Lord God; Come from the four winds, O breath, and breathe upon these slain, that they may live.

10 So I prophesied as he commanded me, and the breath came into them, and they lived, and stood up upon their feet, an exceeding great army.

The miracle took place in two main phases. In the first phase, after Ezekiel preached, the bones were joined together to form skeletons; and flesh then appeared on the bones. This implies that the bones had been scattered. The joining of the bones resulted in a loud noise and a shaking. This may mean that God used an earthquake as an agency or sign of this miracle. Sinews and flesh began to appear on the skeletons. At the end of this process, the dry bones had become bodies covered with flesh. However, at this stage, they were still only dead bodies with no life or breath.

In the second phase, God told Ezekiel to summon the four winds to breathe life into the dead. As God had promised, He put breath into the bodies. The agency of this life-giving breath was the four winds, which were commanded to breathe upon the dead. When the dead received the breath of life, they came alive. They stood up and formed a mighty army of living people instead of a valley of dry bones.

Crucial to this passage is one Hebrew word that can mean "spirit," "breath," or "wind." This word appears a number of times in Ezekiel 37:1–14, and the word is translated in all three ways. The word is translated "breath" in verses 5, 6, 8, 9, 10. It is translated "wind" three times in verse 9. It is translated "spirit" in verses 1 and 14. The root of the word denotes "air in motion," as in wind or breath. The idea of a person's vital breath came to be used of the life-principle or spirit that comes at birth and leaves at death. The word thus also came to be used of the Spirit of God.

Thus, verses 1–14 emphasize that this miracle of making dry bones into living people was possible only by the power of God. As verses 4–6 emphasize the power of God's word, the passage as a whole stresses the power of God's Spirit. The Spirit of God breathes life into the dead, and they come alive.

4. Hope for hopeless Israel (37:11–14)

11 Then he said unto me, Son of man, these bones are the whole house of Israel.

Verses 11–14 explain the meaning and application of the vision of dry bones in verses 1–10. Ezekiel's ministry—like Jeremiah's—fell into two distinct phases: The first phase was before the fall of Jerusalem, and the second was after the fall of Jerusalem. Before the fall of Jerusalem, the people were filled with false hopes of deliverance. This was as true of the exiles in Babylon as of the people in Judah. False prophets promised that God would soon destroy the Babylonians, spare Jerusalem, and liberate the exiles. During those years, Jeremiah in Judah and Ezekiel in Babylon preached sure judgment.

Their prophecies of doom came true when the Babylonians destroyed Jerusalem and the temple in 587 B.C. Then the mood of the people went from false hope to no hope. They felt as helpless and hopeless as a valley of dry bones. Verse 11 quotes them as saying, "Our bones are dried, and our hope is lost." At this point, God began to give Ezekiel messages of hope for the future.

Verses 12–13 change the analogy from dry bones scattered in the open to bodies buried in the ground, but the basic message is the same. God is able to make the dead come alive—whether dry bones in the open or decayed bodies in the grave. Verse 14 emphasizes that God will perform this miracle through His Spirit.

II. Sign of Two Sticks (Ezek. 37:15–28)

1. Two sticks joined (37:15–19)

The Lord often led Ezekiel to use object lessons as prophetic symbols to reinforce His message. God told the prophet to take two sticks and to write "Judah" on one and "Joseph" on the other. ("Joseph" represented the northern tribes, since two important tribes—Ephraim and Manasseh—were two of Joseph's sons. "Joseph" is used here to make clear that one stick represented the scattered northern tribes, since "Israel" was sometimes used to refer to Judah after the fall of Israel.) The prophet was then told to hold the two sticks in his hand to make them appear joined as one stick.

2. Hope for the future (37:20–28)

> 25 And they shall dwell in the land that I have given unto Jacob my servant, wherein your fathers have dwelt.
>
> 26 Moreover I will make a covenant of peace with them; it shall be an everlasting covenant with them: and I will place them, and multiply them, and will set my sanctuary in the midst of them for evermore.
>
> 27 My tabernacle also shall be with them: yea, I will be their God, and they shall be my people.

Jeremiah promised that the exiles would return to the holy land after seventy years (Jer. 29:10), but the promises of Ezekiel 37 looked further into the future than the Old Testament period of restoration.

The symbol of the two sticks joined was a divine promise of the restoration and reunion of people from both northern Israel and southern Judah. The people would be cleansed so they no longer would defile themselves. The one nation would have one King—the one whom God called "David my servant" (37:24). They would follow God's statutes and live forever in the land that the Lord promised to Jacob, and the Messiah would be their prince.

God promised to make with them a covenant of peace. "Peace" is a wholeness that results from reconciliation. Peace with God is primary, but peace with others is inseparable from peace with God. The reunion of Judah and Israel signifies the reconciliation that accompanies the covenant of peace.

The key component of that future age will be a new and permanent relationship with God. God promised to establish His sanctuary in their midst forever. This promise is repeated in verses 26, 27 and 28. Not everyone agrees about when and how this promise will be fulfilled. Many expect a literal fulfillment in an earthly kingdom of God before the new heavens and new earth. Others see these passages as symbolic language to be ful-

November 22, 1998

filled in the eternal new heavens and new earth. Whenever and however God fulfills this promise, the future for God's people is bright with hope.

SUMMARY OF BIBLE TRUTHS

1. People face situations in which they feel helpless and hopeless.
2. God's word and Spirit can cause the dead to live again.
3. God offers hope to the hopeless.
4. The future for believers is as bright as the promises of God.

APPLYING THE BIBLE

1. God can bring victory out of defeat. One of the general principles underlying God's promise to restore Israel is that God can turn the most hopeless situation into victory. He can bring life out of death. His promise to restore Israel is only one illustration of that power, and it is based on His great love for His people.

2. The God who acts. In a moving passage in *Sartor Resartus,* Thomas Carlyle has an interesting picture of the philosopher gazing out across the city at midnight from his lofty attic, musing on the mingled joys and sorrows, hopes and miseries of the one-half million human beings huddled around him there: "But I," he exclaims at last, "I sit above it all; I am alone with the Stars." Is the God of Israel like that? Sitting above it all in deep philosophic thought, distantly removed from the anguish of earthlings? Ezekiel (not to mention every other writer in the Bible) knew differently. He is the God who acts in human history.

3. Creation, providence, consummation. God's restoration of Israel is an expression of His providential care for His people. The three central doctrines of the Bible are creation, providence, and consummation. God made the universe, God sustains the universe, and God will consummate the universe.

4. Our Father is in charge—not fate. The ancient Romans believed there were three goddesses of fate: Clotho held the spindle, Lachesis drew out the thread, and Atropos snipped off the thread at her whimsical will—just as it was supposed that she would snip off one's life. The dictionary defines "fate" as "an inevitable and often adverse outcome, condition, or end." The central concept of fatalism is the idea of inevitability—that we are not in control but are bound in an iron-clad determinism; we are pawns on a cosmic chessboard. That idea is totally foreign to the Bible. Fate is not in control—the Father is!

5. God cares for great and small alike. "God looked down one night and saw two manifestations of trouble on earth. The first involved a king who was sitting in his darkened throne room and was terribly tempted to sin by political compromise. His wrinkled brow betrayed the war in his soul. The other situation involved a lowly ant carrying home a bit of food for its family. A heavy rain had begun to fall, making the trip treacherous. God sent an angel down to 'keep the king from sin and help the ant at entering in'" (source unknown). Ant or king, God cares!

6. How Firm a Foundation. When we think of God's constant care, many of us remember the words of a hymn:

PAGE 94

The soul that on Jesus hath leaned for repose
I will not, I will not desert to his foes;
That soul, though all hell should endeavor to shake,
I'll never, no never, no never forsake!

7. Where is it in your life that you feel helpless and hopeless? Where, if God does not come through in miracle, is victory impossible? Where is it in your life that God must beat the odds? When God asks you, "Son of man, can these bones live?" if you cannot give a resounding yes, at least do what Ezekiel did:

▶ Ezekiel did not dare say no but gently turned the question back to God by saying, "O Lord God, thou knowest;"
▶ Ezekiel obeyed every command of God, no matter how strange they sounded.

TEACHING THE BIBLE

▶ *Main Idea:* God gives hope to those who are hopeless.
▶ *Suggested Teaching Aim*: To lead adults to identify elements of God's hope for their lives.

A TEACHING OUTLINE

God's Vision for Exiles
  I. *Vision of Valley of Dry Bones (Ezek. 37:1–14)*
     1. *Dry bones (37:1–3)*
     2. *Command to preach to the bones (37:4–6)*
     3. *The breath of life (37:7–10)*
     4. *Hope for hopeless Israel (37:11–14)*
  II. *Sign of Two Sticks (Ezek. 37:15–28)*
     1. *Two sticks joined (37:15–19)*
     2. *Hope for the future (37:20–28)*

Introduce the Bible Study
Place a large sheet of paper on the wall. At the top, write in large letters, *As hopeless as . . .* As members enter, ask them to write examples of hopelessness on the sheet of paper. Read these examples to begin the lesson.

Search for Biblical Truth
On a chalkboard write this chart:

Who?	Ezekiel, son of man
What?	A vision of dry bones
When?	Before the fall of Jerusalem
Where?	In Babylonia where he was a captive
Why?	To offer hope

November 22 1998

To establish the background, lecture briefly on these five words, using the ideas in "Studying the Bible." Complete italicized phrases.

Point out that God gave Ezekiel an example of hopelessness that surpassed anything Ezekiel had ever encountered.

Organize the class into four groups of one or more members each and make the following assignments. (If you prefer, you can do this assignment as one large group.)

Group 1. Read Ezekiel 37:1–3 and answer the following questions: (1) Describe Ezekiel's vision. (A battlefield littered with unburied bodies that had had all the flesh eaten off them by the predators and had been bleached by the sun.) (2) What did God ask Ezekiel? (Can these bones live?) (3) What was Ezekiel's answer? (Only God knew the answer.) (4) Who did the dried bones symbolize? (Judah and Israel.)

Group 2. Read Ezekiel 37:4–6 and answer the following questions: (1) What did God ask Ezekiel to do? (Prophesy to the bones.) (2) What did God say He would do to the bones? (Place flesh on them.) (3) What did this symbolize? (That God would give hope to Judah and Israel.)

Group 3. Read Ezekiel 37:7–11 and answer the following questions: (1) What were the two main phases of the miracle? (First the bones were joined and covered with flesh; second, God told Ezekiel to summon the wind to give the bodies breath.) (2) Point out how many times the words *spirit*, *breath*, and *wind* appear in these verses but that they are all the same basic word. ("Breath" in 37:5, 6, 8, 9, 10; "wind" three times in 37:9; "spirit" in 37:1, 14.) (3) What did this symbolize? (Bringing the nation back to life was a miracle performed by God's Spirit.)

Group 4. Read 37:15–27 and answer the following questions: (1) What symbolism did God use in these verses? (Joining two sticks.) (2) What did this symbolize? (Israel and Judah would be joined together.) (3) What did God promise He would do for them in 37:16? (Make a covenant of peace.) (4) What does the promise of the "tabernacle" mean? (May be literal in a new earthly kingdom or symbolic in the eternal new heavens and new earth.)

Give the Truth a Personal Focus

Refer to the sentences that members completed as they entered the room. Say, If you are feeling hopeless, then this lesson can remind you of God's hopefulness. Read the four summary statements from "Summary of Bible Truths."

Distribute paper and pencils. Ask members to write down one aspect of God's hopefulness that will help them.

---

1. James S. Stewart, *Heralds of God* (London: Hodder and Stoughton, 1946), 127.
2. Wilfred Funk, *Word Origins and Their Romantic Stories* (New York: Funk, 1950), 267.

Renewal and Worship

November 29, 1998

Background Passage: Nehemiah 8–9
Focal Passage: Nehemiah 8:13–9:3

Ezra and Nehemiah were the two key personalities of the final period of Old Testament history—the restoration. During that period, significant structures were built—the temple and the wall of Jerusalem. However, of more lasting importance were the religious emphases. Nehemiah 8–9 tells of three religious practices: (1) studying the Law; (2) renewing observance of the worship prescribed in the Law; and (3) confessing sins that led to new commitment.

▶**Study Aim:** *To name and describe three religious emphases of the period of the restoration.*

STUDYING THE BIBLE

OUTLINE AND SUMMARY
  I. **Reading the Law (Neh. 8:1–12)**
      1. **Reading and understanding (8:1–8)**
      2. **Proclaiming a feast of joy (8:9–12)**
  II. **Observing the Feast of Booths (Neh. 8:13–18)**
      1. **Continuing study of the Law (8:13)**
      2. **Discovering a neglected feast (8:14–15)**
      3. **Carefully following the Scriptures (8:16–18)**
  III. **Confessing Sins (Neh. 9:1–38)**
      1. **Fasting, separating, and confessing (9:1–3)**
      2. **Prayer of confession (9:4–37)**
      3. **Making a commitment (9:38)**

Ezra and the Levites read and explained the Law to the people (8:1–8). Ezra, Nehemiah, and the Levites proclaimed a feast of joy (8:9–12). Key leaders continued the study of the Law (8:13). When they found the commands about the Feast of Booths, they sent word for the people to make preparations for it (8:14–15). They observed the feast, being careful to follow all that the Law prescribed (8:16–18). The people fasted, separated themselves from pagans, and confessed sins (9:1–3). The Levites led them in a prayer of confession (9:4–37). The leaders made a renewed commitment (9:38).

I. Reading the Law (Neh. 8:1–12)
1. Reading and understanding (8:1–8)

Just as Judah went into exile in three phases, so did they return to Jerusalem in three stages.
  1. Zerubbabel and Jeshua led the first group back in 538 B.C. After several delays, this first group succeeded in rebuilding the temple.
  2. Ezra led a second group back in 458 B.C. Ezra revived the study of the Law and obedience to it.

November 29 1998

3. Nehemiah led a third group back in 444 B.C. Nehemiah rebuilt the wall around Jerusalem.

Ezra is introduced in Ezra 7–10, but his most significant work is recorded in Nehemiah 8. The people asked Ezra to read the Law to them (8:1). Therefore, all morning on the first day of the seventh month, Ezra read the Law to men, women, and all who could understand (8:2–3). Ezra read from a pulpit built for that purpose (8:4). The people showed their reverence by being attentive, standing, saying "amen," lifting up their hands, bowing their heads, and worshiping with their faces to the ground (8:5–6). The Levites assisted the people in understanding by translating the Hebrew into Aramaic (probably the meaning of "read . . . distinctly") and by interpreting ("gave the sense," 8:7–8).

2. Proclaiming a feast of joy (8:9–12)

The people's initial response was to weep; but Ezra, Nehemiah, and the Levites told the people not to weep (8:9). The leaders called for a feast of joy (8:10). Therefore, the people celebrated because they had understood the words of the Law of God (8:11–12).

II. Observing the Feast of Booths (Neh. 8:13–18)

1. Continuing study of the Law (8:13)

> 13 And on the second day were gathered together the chief of the fathers of all the people, the priests, and the Levites, unto Ezra the scribe, even to understand the words of the law.

The reading to all the people was followed by more intensive study in smaller groups. "The chief of the fathers of all the people" were the leaders, who could return to instruct and guide their tribes, clans, and families. Along with these leaders were the religious leaders—priests and Levites. They wasted no time, for they met on the second day of the month—the day after the reading to all the people.

As on the first day, Ezra the scribe was their teacher. We might use the word *scholar* today. Ezra was "a ready scribe in the law of Moses, which the LORD God of Israel had given" (Ezra 7:6). "Ezra had prepared his heart to seek the law of the LORD, and to do it, and to teach in Israel statutes and judgments" (Ezra 7:10).

These verses affirm three things about Ezra:

1. He was personally devoted to study the Law.
2. His first purpose in studying the Law was in order to obey it himself.
3. His second purpose was to teach the Law to others.

The word translated "understand" in verse 13 means "to cause to act wisely." This is a different word than the one translated "understand" in verses 2, 7, 8, 12, which means "to cause to understand." Both are important. People must understand, but they also must act on that understanding.

2. Discovering a neglected feast (8:14–15)

> 14 And they found written in the law which the LORD had commanded by Moses, that the children of Israel should dwell in booths in the feast of the seventh month:

November 29, 1998

15 And that they should publish and proclaim in all their cities, and in Jerusalem, saying, Go forth unto the mount, and fetch olive branches, and pine branches, and myrtle branches, and branches of thick trees, to make booths, as it is written.

The word *found* implies that they made an important discovery as they studied the Law. They came across one or more of the passages about the Feast of Booths (Tabernacles). The passage was probably Leviticus 23:33–43. One thing that attracted their attention was that the Feast of Booths was to begin on the fifteenth day of the seventh month, and they were studying on the first and second days of the fifteenth month (Neh. 8:2, 13).

Verse 15 describes one action they took as a result of their discovery. The leaders issued a proclamation to observe the Feast of Booths as prescribed by the Law (Lev. 23:40). The people were instructed to gather branches to make booths to live in during the feast. Since the feast was to begin in two weeks, the people had time to gather the branches.

3. Carefully following the Scriptures (8:16–18)

16 So the people went forth, and brought them, and made themselves booths, every one upon the roof of his house, and in their courts, and in the courts of the house of God, and in the street of the water gate, and in the street of the gate of Ephraim.

17 And all the congregation of them that were come again out of the captivity made booths, and sat under the booths: for since the days of Jeshua the son of Nun unto that day had not the children of Israel done so. And there was very great gladness.

18 Also day by day, from the first day unto the last day, he read in the book of the law of God. And they kept the feast seven days; and on the eighth day was a solemn assembly, according unto the manner.

The Feast of Booths had a twofold purpose. (1) It was a harvest festival (Exod. 34:22). (2) It reminded the children of Israel of the Lord's care of them during their years in the wilderness, when they lived in temporary dwellings (Lev. 23:42–43). The booths were to remind them of the Lord's gracious provision for them during those years and of the land to which he was leading them, in which they would dwell in houses.

This is another reason that the Feast of Booths caught their attention. Like their forefathers, they had emerged from years of captivity. This is spelled out in the first part of verse 17. They saw their deliverance from Babylonia as a new exodus and their return to Judah as a new entry into the promised land.

The last part of verse 17 has puzzled Bible students because it seems to say that this was the first observance of the Feast of Booths since the time of Joshua (usual spelling of "Jeshua"). However, the Bible records an observance of this feast in Ezra 3:4. The point, therefore, is that this was the first time since Joshua when such care was given to ensure that everything that the Law required was done.

Verse 18 reinforces that explanation of verse 17. They continued to search the Law for any mention of the Feast of Booths. Then they were careful to do everything prescribed in the Law. They kept the feast for seven days and the eighth day as a solemn assembly as required by the Law (Lev. 23:36, Num. 29:35).

The Book of Nehemiah presents Ezra's emphasis on the Law. This became a distinctive emphasis of the Jewish people that continued into future centuries. The Jews became a people of the Book.

III. Confessing Sins (Neh. 9:1–38)

1. **Fasting, separating, and confessing (9:1–3)**

> 1 Now in the twenty and fourth day of this month the children of Israel were assembled with fasting, and with sackclothes, and earth upon them.
>
> 2 And the seed of Israel separated themselves from all strangers, and stood and confessed their sins, and the iniquities of their fathers.
>
> 3 And they stood up in their place, and read in the book of the law of the LORD their God one fourth part of the day; and another fourth part they confessed, and worshipped the LORD their God.

That was a busy month! Two days after the solemn assembly, they assembled again for fasting. They came wearing sackcloth and with dirt on their heads. These were all signs of great distress, often of sorrow for sin. Fasting was not new to the Old Testament, but it came to be even more important during the years after the Exile.

Separation from unbelieving pagans had been commanded by the Lord throughout Israel's history. Their failure to do so had been a key factor in the moral compromise and idolatry that finally sent them into exile. Now they had learned that lesson. The period after the Exile was a time when Jews developed their distinctive practices and avoided unnecessary contacts with pagans. This issue was crucial in this period as leaders challenged the people to take drastic actions (see Ezra 10–11; Neh. 13).

Most of Nehemiah 9 has to do with the people confessing their sins. We may wonder why they first rejoiced (8:9–12) and then confessed their sins. Even before they rejoiced, they were feeling the weight of their guilt. The Law in the Old Testament led to both these responses: (1) It led to conviction and confession; (2) it was a source of joy.

Verse 3 shows that the study of the Law continued to be the driving force behind these actions. They spent one fourth of the day studying the Law and another fourth confessing their sins and worshiping the Lord. Most churches continue this pattern in the Sunday meetings for Bible study and worship.

2. **Prayer of confession (9:4–37)**

The Old Testament contains several prayers of confession of sins. This is one of the longest ones. The Levites led the people in this confession. The twofold theme of the prayer is (1) the persistent sinning of Israel and (2) the longsuffering mercy and goodness of God. Like Psalm 78, the prayer moves through history. As verse 2 notes, "They confessed their sins, and the iniquities of their fathers."

The prayer contains the following parts: Praise to God as Creator (9:6), the covenant with Abraham (9:7–8), the great and wonderful acts of God in Egypt (9:9–11), God's care and leadership (9:12), Mount Sinai and the wilderness (9:13–21), the conquest of the promised land (9:22–25), Israel's unfaithfulness and God's patience (9:26–31), and confession of sin and plea for mercy (9:32–37).

3. Making a commitment (9:38)

Following their confession of sins, the leaders renewed their commitment to the Lord.

SUMMARY OF BIBLE TRUTHS

1. Study of the Scriptures ought to lead to new understanding and insights.
2. Serious study of the Scriptures leads to obedience to God's Word.
3. Joyful and grateful worship is one result of serious study of God's Word.
4. Confessing sins is another result.

APPLYING THE BIBLE

1. Bible truth changes lives. Dwight L. Moody once said, "The Lord did not give us the Bible to increase our knowledge, but to change our lives." The book of Nehemiah is a prime biblical example of God's people understanding what Moody said. The emphasis of Nehemiah's preaching was that truth blesses the body politic. Beyond that (and, certainly, in connection with it) God's truth, applied positively and redemptively, affects individuals.

2. Applied Christianity. Williams S. Sadler, a Chicago psychiatrist, said it like this: "If Christianity were practically applied to our everyday life, it would so purify and vitalize the race that at least one-half of our sickness and sorrow would disappear. Faith is an actual remedy for those physical ills which result from doubt, depression, and discouragement. I make this statement as a physician and surgeon. Fear is the cause of the worry and nervousness which are responsible for most of the functional diseases."[1]

3. The truth requires action. To quote Moody again, he once said that the church's biggest problem is "trafficking in unlived truth." And Vance Havner offered a keen insight about the response of those who heard Peter's heart-piercing sermon recorded in Acts 2. They did not, he said, respond by saying, "Is there a motion on the floor that we accept this as information to be considered?" but "Men and brethren, what shall we do (to be saved)?" (Acts 2:37).

4. Thoughts on confession. The response of the people of God in Nehemiah's day centered on the confession of their sins. People have found this true through the ages:

November 29 1998

- "The confession of evil works is the first beginning of good works" (Augustine).
- "Confession of sin puts the soul under the blessing of God" (Anonymous).
- "It is an abuse to confess any kind of sin, whether mortal or venial, without a will to be delivered from it, since confession was instituted for no other end" (Francis of Sales).
- "There is no refuge from confession but suicide; and suicide is confession" (Daniel Webster).
- "He that covereth his sins shall not prosper but whoso confesseth and forsaketh them shall have mercy" (Prov. 28:13). Can we obtain mercy if we do only one of the two prescribed acts—confessing sin and forsaking sin? Why?

It is far more difficult to repent of the sin one is planning to commit in the future than the sin he has committed in the past!

5. God calls a separated people. Nehemiah's people separated themselves from evil practices. See the references to separation in 9:2, 10:28, and 13:3. He who is serious about pleasing God—and enjoying His blessing—must give us certain practices. And philosophies. And pleasures. And people. On the idea of separation, see 2 Corinthians 6:14–18. In 1 Thessalonians 1:9, the double emphasis of all biblical separation is emphasized—one must move away from his sin and then to God. We are to separate *from* some things and *to* some things; to do either one without the other misses the blessing. "For they themselves shew of us what manner of entering in we had unto you, and how ye turned to God from idols to serve the living and true God" (1 Thess. 1:9).

6. Breaking free from bad companions. "Never break off a friendship, rather untie it, when those you become bound to appear cheats." Hall says, "I will use my friend as Moses did his rod: while it was a rod he held it familiarly in his hand: when once a serpent, he ran away from it."[2] Ask yourself these questions:

- Have you ever had to break off a friendship because it had become detrimental to your spiritual development?
- Is it possible that you need to separate from some practice, some philosophy, some pleasure, some person or people?
- What precise steps would you counsel a Christian to take in the separation process?
- Why is separation so difficult?

7. Evil influences. First Corinthians 15 is the magnificent chapter on the resurrection, but tucked away in verse 33 of this chapter is important thought on companionships: "Be not deceived: evil communications corrupt good manners." The verse is rather difficult in the King James Version, but listen to how others put it:

- "Bad company ruins good morals" (NRSV).
- "Bad company corrupts good morals" (NASB).
- "Bad company corrupts good character" (NLT).

For an illustration from the world of nature, discuss that old adage your mom told you a hundred times, "Birds of a feather flock together." My surrogate father, my brother-in-law—even though at the time he was not a Christian—once told me a chilling truth, "Bill, all your buddies are bums!" He's in paradise now, and I hope he knows how much I appreciate his telling me that painful truth, even though I didn't act on it immediately!

November 29 1998

TEACHING THE BIBLE

▶ *Main Idea:* Studying the Bible should lead us to grateful worship and humble confession of our sins.
▶ *Suggested Teaching Aim:* To lead adults to identify steps they can take to renewal and worship.

A TEACHING OUTLINE

Renewal and Worship

I. *Reading the Law (Neh. 8:1–12)*
  1. *Reading and understanding (8:1–8)*
  2. *Proclaiming a feast of joy (8:9–12)*
II. *Observing the Feast of Booths (Neh. 8:13–18)*
  1. *Continuing study of the Law (8:13)*
  2. *Discovering a neglected feast (8:14–15)*
  3. *Carefully following the Scriptures (8:16–18)*
III. *Confessing Sins (Neh. 9:1–38)*
  1. *Fasting, separating, and confessing (9:1–3)*
  2. *Prayer of confession (9:4–37)*
  3. *Making a commitment (9:38)*

Introduce the Bible Study

Read this statement by Dwight L. Moody from "Applying the Bible": "The Lord did not give us the Bible to increase our knowledge, but to change our lives." Point out that today's lesson describes how reading God's Word changes lives.

Search for Biblical Truth

Point out that Nehemiah 8–9 tells of three religious practices: (1) Studying the Law; (2) renewing observance of the worship prescribed in the Law; and (3) confessing sins that led to new commitment.
IN ADVANCE, make the following poster:

Israel's Return from Exile
1. Zerubbabel and Jeshua led the first returnees in 538 B.C.
2. Ezra led a second group back in 458 B.C.
3. Nehemiah led a third group back in 444 B.C.